Building on SugarCRM

Building on SugarCRM

John Mertic

O'REILLY®

Beijing · Cambridge · Farnham · Köln · Sebastopol · Tokyo

Building on SugarCRM
by John Mertic

Published by O'Reilly Media, Inc., 1005 Gravenstein Highway North, Sebastopol, CA 95472.

O'Reilly books may be purchased for educational, business, or sales promotional use. Online editions are also available for most titles (*http://my.safaribooksonline.com*). For more information, contact our corporate/institutional sales department: (800) 998-9938 or *corporate@oreilly.com*.

Editor: Julie Steele
Production Editor: O'Reilly Publishing Services

Cover Designer: Karen Montgomery
Interior Designer: David Futato
Illustrator: O'Reilly Publishing Services

Printing History:

July 2011:	First Edition.

ISBN: 978-1-449-30980-0

[LSI]

1310752032

Table of Contents

Preface

Conventions Used in This Book

Italic

Indicates new terms, URLs, email addresses, filenames, and file extensions.

`Constant width`

Used for program listings.

 This icon signifies a tip, suggestion, or general note.

Using Code Examples

This book is here to help you get your job done. In general, you may use the code in this book in your programs and documentation. You do not need to contact us for permission unless you're reproducing a significant portion of the code. For example, writing a program that uses several chunks of code from this book does not require permission. Selling or distributing a CD-ROM of examples from O'Reilly books does require permission. Answering a question by citing this book and quoting example code does not require permission. Incorporating a significant amount of example code from this book into your product's documentation does require permission.

We appreciate, but do not require, attribution. An attribution usually includes the title, author, publisher, and ISBN. For example: "*Building on SugarCRM* by John Mertic (O'Reilly). Copyright 2011 SugarCRM Inc., 978-1-449-30980-0."

If you feel your use of code examples falls outside fair use or the permission given above, feel free to contact us at *permissions@oreilly.com*.

Safari® Books Online

Safari Books Online is an on-demand digital library that lets you easily search over 7,500 technology and creative reference books and videos to find the answers you need quickly.

With a subscription, you can read any page and watch any video from our library online. Read books on your cell phone and mobile devices. Access new titles before they are available for print, and get exclusive access to manuscripts in development and post feedback for the authors. Copy and paste code samples, organize your favorites, download chapters, bookmark key sections, create notes, print out pages, and benefit from tons of other time-saving features.

O'Reilly Media has uploaded this book to the Safari Books Online service. To have full digital access to this book and others on similar topics from O'Reilly and other publishers, sign up for free at *http://my.safaribooksonline.com*.

How to Contact Us

Please address comments and questions concerning this book to the publisher:

O'Reilly Media, Inc.
1005 Gravenstein Highway North
Sebastopol, CA 95472
800-998-9938 (in the United States or Canada)
707-829-0515 (international or local)
707-829-0104 (fax)

We have a web page for this book, where we list errata, examples, and any additional information. You can access this page at:

http://www.oreilly.com/catalog/9781449309800

To comment or ask technical questions about this book, send email to:

bookquestions@oreilly.com

For more information about our books, courses, conferences, and news, see our website at *http://www.oreilly.com*.

Find us on Facebook: *http://facebook.com/oreilly*

Follow us on Twitter: *http://twitter.com/oreillymedia*

Watch us on YouTube: *http://www.youtube.com/oreillymedia*

CHAPTER 1

What is SugarCRM?

SugarCRM is the world's largest open source CRM (customer relationship management) software. Founded in 2004, over 7,000 customers and more than half a million users rely on SugarCRM to execute marketing programs, grow sales, retain customers, and create custom business applications. These custom business applications can be used in a multitude of ways, such as to power sales teams, run customer support organizations, and manage customer information databases.

One of the unique things about SugarCRM in the CRM space is that it's fundamentally an open source application, meaning that the source code of the application is available to any user, developer, or customer of the product. Whether one opts for the AGPLv3 licensed or the commercially licensed version, the application comes with all of the source code, enabling developers to customize and build upon the product with ease. This puts the control of your application and your data in your hands, enabling the freedom to deploy SugarCRM wherever you wish. This ability has given SugarCRM partners and developers worldwide the ability to customize the out-of-the-box application to fit in many different organizations, vertical markets, and locales.

But before we dig in deeper to how you could take the SugarCRM platform and build upon it, let's take a peek at the various editions of SugarCRM, how and where we can deploy SugarCRM, and some of the components that come with SugarCRM out of the box to enable you to build applications with ease.

A breakdown of the editions

The latest version of SugarCRM as of this writing is 6.2, released in June 2011. For this version we expanded the number of editions of the product from three to five, to better cover the various demographics of our customers and better streamline our product support offerings, as well as provide new add-on products to complement the base product.

Community Edition

Community Edition is released under the AGPLv3 license. The Community Edition and related extensions have been downloaded over 8 million times since 2004. This edition comes fully featured with all the basics for sales, marketing, support automation, and user and ACL management, as well as the developer tools Studio and Module Builder for customizing the application. It can be downloaded from *http://www.sugarforge.org/content/downloads/*.

Professional Edition

Professional Edition is a commercial edition of the product that builds upon the feature set of the Community Edition. Of these numerous additional features added to Professional Edition, the most notable are:

- Support for Teams, where users can be grouped together by their department or job function.
- A reporting tool enabling you to run several different types of reports, many of which have charts with them that can be added to the Home page
- A web-based mobile version, along with mobile clients specific for the iPhone and Android smart phones
- Plug-ins for Microsoft Office, namely Outlook, Word, and Excel

Corporate Edition

This is a new edition of the product added with the Sugar 6.2 release, which adds additional features on top of the Sugar Professional feature set:

- An enhanced mobile client with offline storage capabilities for the iPhone, iPad, and Blackberry platforms
- A higher level of customer support

Enterprise Edition

Enterprise Edition is targeted at large organizations and builds upon the Professional and Corporate Editions with additional features:

- A more robust reporting tool
- An offline client for desktop use
- Self-service portal, which enables you to deploy a portal that your customers can use to interact with your Sugar instance with ease
- Sugar Plug-in for Lotus Notes
- Support for the Oracle database

- An even higher level of customer support

Ultimate Edition

This is the most feature-complete edition of SugarCRM, and is also a new offering with Sugar 6.2. In addition to all the features in the other editions, this edition adds:

- Sugar Connector for Lotus Domino Server
- Our highest level of customer support

What you need to install SugarCRM

Because of SugarCRM's roots as a LAMP (Linux Apache MySQL PHP) application, it is quite easy to get a basic install of SugarCRM up and running. All you need to get going is the following software stack:

- A computer (either Unix or Windows OSs supported)
- A web server (Apache 2.x or IIS 6 and 7.x are supported)
- A database (MySQL 5.x, SQL Server 2005/2008, or Oracle 10g/11g)
- A recent version of PHP configured to work with the above components (both PHP 5.2 or 5.3 are supported)
- A web browser to access the application (IE 7/8, Firefox, Safari, and Chrome are supported)

If you are running a recent Linux distribution, all of these components should be readily be available through your distribution's package manager (deb, rpm, etc). On Windows, a great way to get the whole stack installed is through the Microsoft Web Platform installer, including SugarCRM itself (see *http://www.microsoft.com/web/*). And we also provide full stack installers as well for Windows, Linux, and OS X, which include a web server, database, PHP, and SugarCRM all ready to go for ease of installation.

The application installer for SugarCRM is web-based, so all you need to do is unzip the downloaded package somewhere in your web server root, navigate to the location you unzipped the file with your web browser, and follow the step-by-step instructions. This makes it very simple to get an instance up and running quickly, and means you don't need any special hardware if you just want to check out SugarCRM and play with it.

How about running in the cloud?

One of the biggest gains in having such simple deployment requirements is that you can easily install SugarCRM anywhere these components exist. So while for some that may mean installing SugarCRM on a machine in your server closet or data canter, others may not want the overhead of purchasing or maintaining hardware. This is a growing trend in IT, and has resulted in growth of a concept called "Cloud Computing," where the applications physically reside in a shared data canter far away and you access the application instance over the Internet. This can provide an organization huge cost savings over hosting the application themselves and dealing with the hardware and personnel costs of doing so (not having to buy server hardware, not needing extra IT staff to maintain the servers, etc).

SugarCRM was designed from the beginning with this in mind. By relying on the LAMP stack, you can deploy on any platform that provides those components, even cloud-based ones. Customers have deployed SugarCRM very successfully on cloud platforms such as IBM Cloud, Amazon EC2, Rackspace, and others. And as part of any commercial edition licensing, you can run SugarCRM on Sugar's own cloud at no extra charge where they will maintain and handle upgrades of SugarCRM.

There isn't a cloud that's a stranger to SugarCRM.

What do you get with SugarCRM?

Above you learned all about the various editions of SugarCRM and the differences between them. As you can infer, the biggest changes between the editions revolve around additions to the product (such as external integration products, extra support, or additional modules). This means that the core parts of the product are virtually the same between all the various editions of the product. This design is intentional, as we want the most robust and stable platform to build the features our customers need to keep their organizations running. The advantage for developers is that you can use these base-level components as a platform for building any sort of application.

Let's take a quick look at what features SugarCRM provides to make it an ideal platform on which to build.

Modular design

The application is designed to be modular by its very nature, which is a good design paradigm for any software platform. Each part of the application, whether it's account management, contact management, calendaring, or campaigns, is its own module. These modules can interact with one another through data relationships. For example, an account can have many associated contacts with it, or a call can be scheduled for a contact.

The beauty of the Sugar platform is that you can build upon this base by customizing these modules by adding new fields, additional relationships between modules, and business logic. And you can take things a step further and easily design new modules using Module Builder based upon common module design templates, or a clean slate with custom-built forms and relationships. By keeping a modular design, it makes it easier to customize and build the application exactly how you need it, and at the same time leverage all the existing functionality the platform offers.

MVC Framework

MVC, which stands for Model View Controller, is the primary design pattern for web-based applications today. The reason for this is in its simplicity; by keeping your development assets in a defined area, it makes the overall structure and flow of your application cleaner and clearer. It does this by enforcing a separation of business logic and presentation logic, and having a layer in between them that handles the communication and flow of the application as a whole. Figure 1-1 visualizes this pattern.

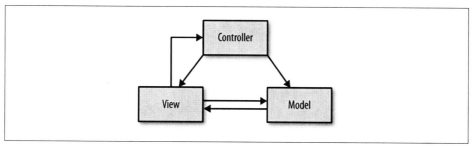

Figure 1-1. Diagram of the Model View Controller paradigm

SugarCRM leverages this design pattern as the primary request flow in the application. Inside the platform, each module provides a primary controller, which handles the incoming requests and deals with them correctly, directing them to views, which handle the presentation logic. And each module also provides one or more model classes that handle the interaction between the application and the data store underneath, whether that be a traditional database, web service, or some other sort of data store. We'll dig more into how you can customize and work with this in the examples in Chapter 4.

Metadata-Driven Views

One common thread that often appears with many business applications is that the same kinds of views (or screens) are used over and over again. This is especially true with SugarCRM, as the primary views a user works with are those for creating and editing a record, viewing the details of a record, and searching on and listing the records available in a module. But these views certainly aren't static, as each module and each user expects different fields with different characteristics to be available. Using the approach of straight HTML forms for each would create a severe code maintenance and quality issue, as on the back end we'd have lots of copying and pasting of templates all over the place, which results in sloppy code and bugs.

We were running into this same issue back before SugarCRM 5 a few years back, so we chose to remedy the situation by implementing metadata-driven views. This allows you to define the fields to be displayed in the given form and some characteristics of them, such as the field label or custom parameters to be passed to the underlying HTML content.

Then this metadata is taken and used to build a dynamic HTML form that is defined as a template, so that it understands the given metadata format and can build the resulting HTML content to be returned to the browser. This process makes it much easier to customize and build forms, removing the need for digging into the details of HTML markup to build common forms.

This process also enables easier customization of forms using other tools, making it possible to edit these forms through Studio and Module Builder without having to touch code at all. We'll learn more about these tools in Chapter 2.

User Authentication and Access Control

Probably the most important part of any multi-user application is how to make sure access to the application and the stored data is secure and well protected. Data security issues have become one of the biggest challenges any IT department faces these days, and the threat is not only from outside attackers, but also from regular users of the application. This puts the pressure on developers to add sophisticated security features, which can be difficult to implement properly in an extensible way.

Roles » Customer Support Administrator

| Edit | Duplicate | Delete |

| Name: | Customer Support Administrator |
| Description: | Customer Support Administrator Role |

Double click on a cell to change value.

All | Save | Cancel |

	Access	Access Type	Delete	Edit
Sponsors	Enabled	Admin & Developer	Not Set	Not Set
Bug Tracker	Enabled	Admin & Developer	Not Set	Not Set
Calls	Not Set	Not Set	Not Set	Not Set
Campaigns	Not Set	Not Set	Not Set	Not Set
Cases	Enabled	Admin & Developer	Not Set	Not Set
Sponsor Contacts	Enabled	Admin & Developer	Not Set	Not Set
Contracts	Not Set	Not Set	Not Set	Not Set
Documents	Not Set	Not Set	Not Set	Not Set
External Accounts	Not Set	Not Set	Not Set	Not Set

Sidebar list: All, Sponsors, Bug Tracker, Calls, Cases, Sponsor Contacts, Contracts, Documents, External Accounts, Leads, Meetings, Notes, Notifications, Sponsorships

Figure 1-2. Role Access Control Management in SugarCRM

SugarCRM, being designed from the ground up as a multi-user business application, comes with advanced data and application security out of the box. You can define users with login credentials in the system (that can also tie back into an existing LDAP or other type of authentication system) to restrict access to the application as a whole. Each user then can have multiple role permissions applied to them, so you can have fine-grained control over the areas of an application a user can access.

This is further strengthened in the commercial editions, where Team support and field-level ACLs (access control lists) allow administrators to more effectively manage large numbers of users with very low-level control over how they can interact with the application. So for example, you could have data entry people only allowed to edit records in a module assigned to them, making all other records effectively read-only in the process. Or, you could define administrators for certain areas of the application (say for Account and Contact management) yet not allow those administrators to administrate other areas of the application that they shouldn't be allowed to.

External Services Integration

It's a wide wide world, and this is so very true when it comes to the software world. There are lots of web services, legacy applications, or other tools that contain data we want to get after and use. We've seen this theme emerging, and have built frameworks inside of SugarCRM to make this easy to leverage in a universal way.

The first way is through the Connectors framework. This framework enables you to add in-record, on-demand integrations to external Web services with ease. By default we include integration with LinkedIn, the popular professional social network, which allows you to look up information about the various people and organizations stored in your SugarCRM application. Other integrations to InsideView and Hoovers come with the different editions of SugarCRM, and developers have built additional integrations using the Connectors framework with Google, Twitter, and many other services.

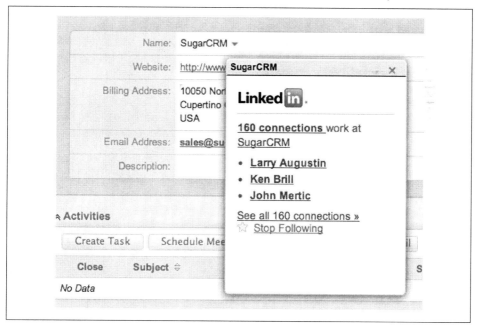

Figure 1-3. LinkedIn Connector

We then added a secondary way of doing more in-depth integrations using a specific API, which can better consume content of these applications and services. This has enabled integrations to services using OAuth and other forms of Authentication, such as Twitter, Facebook, and WebEx. This API is very extensible to allow developers to add the logic for connecting to other services and leverage them directly inside SugarCRM. We'll look at some examples of building this kind of integration in Chapter 5.

Web Services API

Just as you are able to connect to outside services from within SugarCRM, you can also connect back to your SugarCRM instance via Web services. Web services are a way that you can interact with an application over the HTTP protocol. SugarCRM provides support for the two most popular web service protocol standards: SOAP and REST.

Web services provide a clean, non-invasive way to interact with your SugarCRM. You can do just about anything a normal user could do in SugarCRM via the web services API, including adding new records, editing existing records, deleting records, and searching for records by a given criteria. These operations are valid for any module provided with SugarCRM by default, and are also available with custom created modules and fields. We'll look into how to work with this API in Chapter 5.

Ease of Administration

The most forgotten part of any application is the administration interface. I find this the most important piece of an application, since this makes an administrator's life much easier for the common tasks they need to accomplish on a regular basis. It also can help streamline maintenance of the application, as you can have simple forms to handle tasks that would be quite complex otherwise.

Figure 1-4. Administration panel

SugarCRM has an entire administration section, and with access control limits, you can control which users can access this and for which modules the user has access to. And if you build custom modules, you can also add administration panels for controlling the features of them.

Easy to use developer tools

Since most people don't want to have to dig into source code or configuration files when they need to change or modify the fields or layouts in the application, we've created a few different GUI tools to simplify the process. These tools make most common customizations you'll do in SugarCRM very simple.

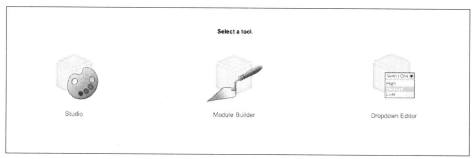

Figure 1-5. SugarCRM Developer Tools

Here's the breakdown of the GUI tools provided in SugarCRM:

- *Studio* is a tool for modifying the out-of-the-box modules, enabling adding and editing fields, changing layouts, and adding new relationships to other modules. The commercial editions of SugarCRM also contain a support for Sugar Logic, which is a way to easily create calculated field values and control field visibility based on formulas that can be built with a GUI-based Formula Editor (we'll see how this in action in Chapter 3).

- *Module Builder* enables you to build new modules, which you can deploy on the current instance or package up for deployment on a different SugarCRM instance.

- *Sugar Portal Editor* (Enterprise and Ultimate Editions only) allows you to customize the self-service portal

- *Dropdown Editor* allows you to edit the display fields and database values for the various dropdown fields used throughout the application.

- *Workflow* allows you to create business logic actions when a record is created or changed in a defined way.

We'll learn more about these tools in Chapter 2, and put them in action in Chapter 3.

Upgrade safeness

I've implemented and integrated with various software solutions many times in my 10+ years of software development experience, both with open source and commercial products. The biggest pain I've always run into is making changes to the application safely; often times I've had customizations broken or overwritten, sometimes causing problems throughout the application. I've even had software packages I've refused to upgrade because of the customizations, and as a result lose out on all the fixes and updates provided by newer versions.

SugarCRM takes upgrade-safeness seriously, providing a multitude of ways to make customizations to the application without causing pain when you are upgrading the base product. You will see with the work we do in Chapters 4 and 5, all the code created is put in a special area set aside for developer customization, and we don't alter it during the upgrade process.

Summary

In this chapter, we looked at a brief overview of SugarCRM, considering the various editions of the product and deployment options. We then looked at the various platform features that make SugarCRM such a compelling platform to build an application on top of.

Now that we have some background on SugarCRM, let's dig more into the developer tools of SugarCRM, and how we can use them in helping to use SugarCRM as a platform for building applications.

CHAPTER 2

Developing on the SugarCRM platform

As we saw back in Chapter 1, the SugarCRM has lots to offer a developer. With a robust, modern MVC platform, convenient features, and a customizable and extensible framework, SugarCRM can be easily bent and twisted to solve whatever needs your organization has. This is what sets SugarCRM apart from its competitors in the CRM space, and what makes it such an ideal platform to build upon.

When most of us think of "developing an application," we immediately want to jump into a text editor and start whipping up code. This is quite a barrier for most people, as for most business people, the language of PHP code is Greek to them, and bringing on a full staff of developers is not something they want to get themselves into for most simple tasks (there are more complex tasks in Chapters 4 and 5 where having a good PHP developer is helpful). So when the idea of "customizing an application to meet your needs" is brought up, you can imagine why most people shudder at the thought.

At SugarCRM, we've realized this, and so we've built several GUI-based developer tools right into the product that make doing much of the customization for a SugarCRM instance easy. In this chapter, we'll look at some of those tools and how to navigate through them, and in Chapter 4 we'll use them to build an application on the SugarCRM platform. We'll begin our survey of these tools by looking at Studio.

Customizing the out-of-the-box modules with Studio

Studio allows you to make basic customizations to the modules that are provided by SugarCRM out of the box, by editing the layouts, subpanels, fields, and labels to align with your business and processes. It's the go-to tool for quickly modifying the out-of-the-box experience for your SugarCRM instance, allowing you to customize the modules without any programming knowledge.

The UI for Studio is very AJAX-driven, where the main panel has the contents of the current action you are working on and the left-side panel is a tree view of the available modules and the items you can edit. Let's step through some of the things you can do.

Figure 2-1. Main Screen for Studio

Adding and changing fields

The most common task people do in Studio is adding and changing fields for a module. To start off with, click the 'Fields' link under any module, which brings you to a view listing all the fields available in the module.

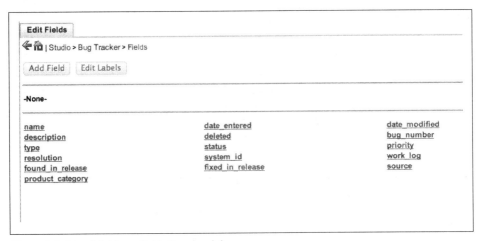

Figure 2-2. List of fields available for a module

You can click on any field to bring up the properties for it. You can do quite a bit of adjusting of the field here, like changing the size, the label, and the default value, whether it's a required field for the module or not, and even more depending upon the field type. Once you are done changing the field, just click 'Save' and the changes will be deployed instantly to your SugarCRM instance.

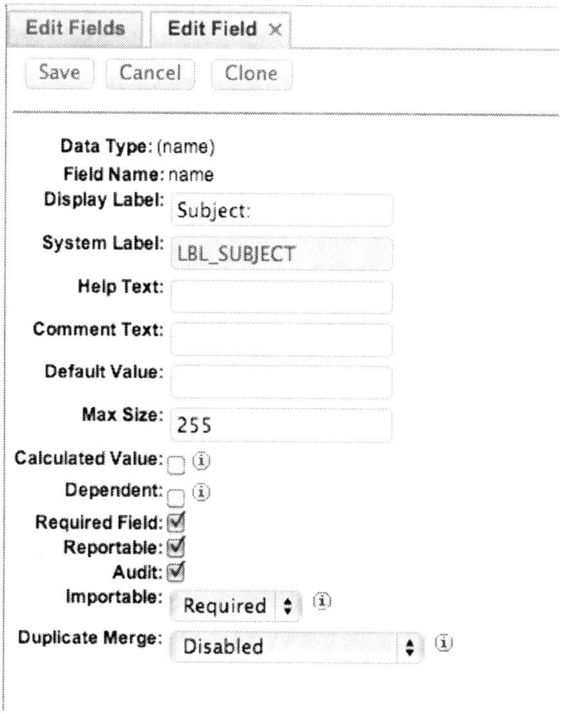

Figure 2-3. Editing a field in Studio

If you want to add additional fields to the module, you can click on the 'Add Field' link at the top of the listing of fields available in your module. This will bring up a similar field editing dialog as before, but in this case you can also specify the type of field you wish to use and the field's database name. SugarCRM comes with the most common field types out of the box, including textual, numeric, currency, dropdown, and multiselect field types. More field types can also be added through custom PHP coding.

Again, just as we did above when editing an existing field, you can simply provide the information for your field and click 'Save' to add the field to the module in realtime. Do note that this just adds the field to the module only, and not the EditView, Detail-View, or any other view by default. We'll see later on in this chapter on how to add it to any of the layout forms.

Building custom business logic with Sugar Logic

One new feature in Sugar 6 in the commercial editions is the Sugar Logic engine, which allows you to easily add business logic to a module. With Sugar Logic, you can define formulas and rules that can be executed on both the server-side as well as directly in

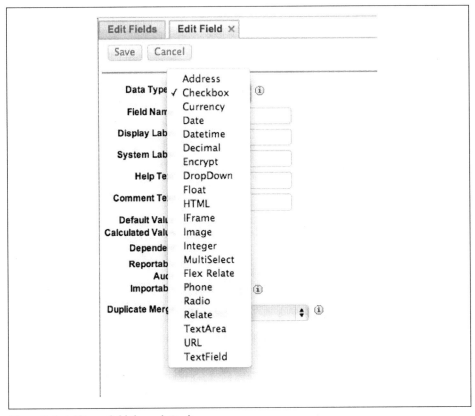

Figure 2-4. Adding a field through Studio

the browser. This enables adding dynamic functionality to forms, such as adding built-in calculations inside forms or hiding and showing fields based upon certain field conditions being met. Studio exposes two forms of doing this: calculated fields and dependent dropdowns.

A Calculated Value field is one in which a formula determines the field value, enabling you to calculate data automatically based on user input. You can use any available field in the module for which you are creating the Calculated Value field. A formula specifies one or more field values along with operators and functions that are mathematical or logical. When you execute a formula, Sugar performs the calculation to derive the value. When a field is used in a formula, Sugar recalculates the value whenever a user updates it and saves the record. Similarly, if you update a formula, Sugar recalculates the field value based on the updated formula. You can also use a Calculated Value field in formulas for other Calculated Value fields, and also in workflows and reports. Any changes you make to the value of the original field, manually or through a workflow, are reflected in the calculated field on the selected tabs of the layout.

The Sugar Logic syntax is designed to be very similar to how Excel formulas work, making the learning curve for business users lower. To create these formulas, just click on the 'Calculated Value' checkbox and then click on the 'Edit Formula' button to bring up the Formula Editor window.

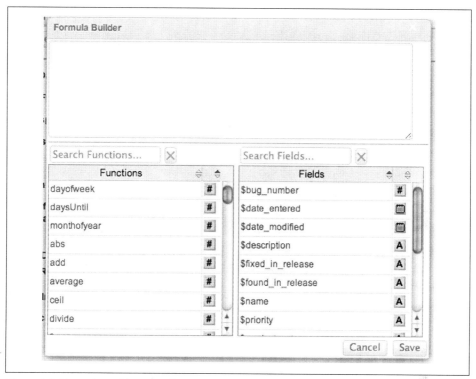

Figure 2-5. Formula Builder in Studio

You can simply click on the functions and fields to build the logic you need to calculate what the value of this field should be.

The other option in the UI is building dependent fields. This allows you to specify the logic for determining whether or not the field should be visible in the layout of the form, based upon the values of other fields in the form. To make this field dependent, you can checkbox 'Dependent', and then put in the logic via Formula Builder for determining if the field should be visible or not.

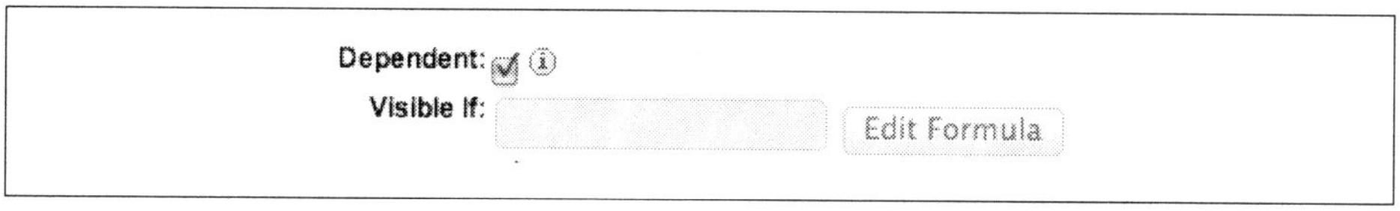

Figure 2-6.

We'll take a more in-depth look at building Sugar Logic formulas through the examples in Chapter 3.

Changing view field layouts

Once you've added or changed fields in a module, the next logical thing to do is to adjust the view layouts accordingly to accommodate them. With Studio, you can adjust all of the metadata-driven views in the product with the ease of a drag-and-drop interface. These views include:

- Creating or editing a record (EditView)
- Details of a record (DetailView)
- Listing of records for a module (ListView)
- Search fields available for a module (Search)
- Short form for creating a record in a popup window or inline in a subpanel (Quick-Create)
- Layout of the popup selector for records in the module (PopupView)
- Search and list fields for the Dashlet based upon the module (Sugar Dashlet)
- Field layout for the Subpanel listing of records
- Layouts of the views of a record in mobile clients (such as iPhone, Android, or the web-based mobile client)

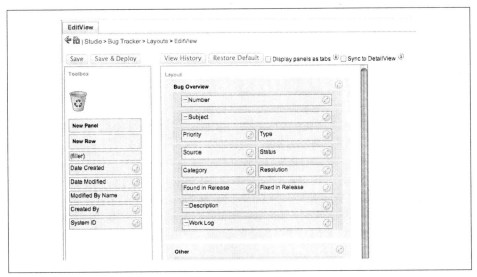

Figure 2-7. Editing the EditView for a record through Studio

For EditViews, DetailView, and QuickCreates, you can simply drag the fields listed in the 'Toolbox' section into the 'Layout' panel, dropping them into empty areas of the form. The forms by default have a two-column layout, but you can stretch a field out across two fields if you wish. If you need to add new rows to the layout, you can do so by dropping in the 'New Row' item into the 'Layout' area. You can even add new panels by dragging the 'New Panel' item over, which is nice to pull groups of related fields together into one section. You can also use this as the basis for having multiple tabs of information for a record by clicking the 'Display panels as tabs' option.

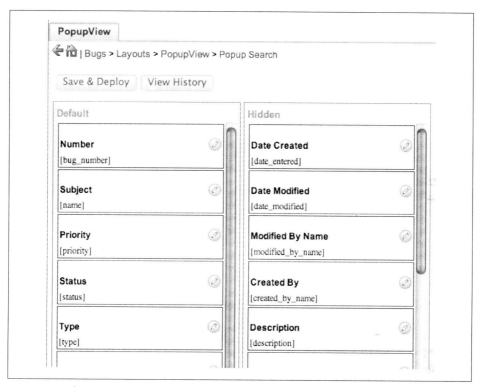

Figure 2-8. Editing the fields available for the PopupView Search through Studio

All of the other views (Search, ListView, PopupView, Subpanels) have simpler column approach, where you can drag the items over from the 'Hidden' column to the 'Default' or 'Available' one to make the items able to be searched upon. 'Default' means the records show up by default in the order listed, while 'Available' means the user can configure their instance to show those fields optionally ('Available' is on ListViews only).

Add new module relationships

One of the best properties of SugarCRM is that you can have records related to one another. This enables you to be able to display and pull together related records very easily on reports and on displays of the records.

Relationships are very easy to create using Studio; just click the 'Relationships' item underneath the module to show all the available relationships in the module.

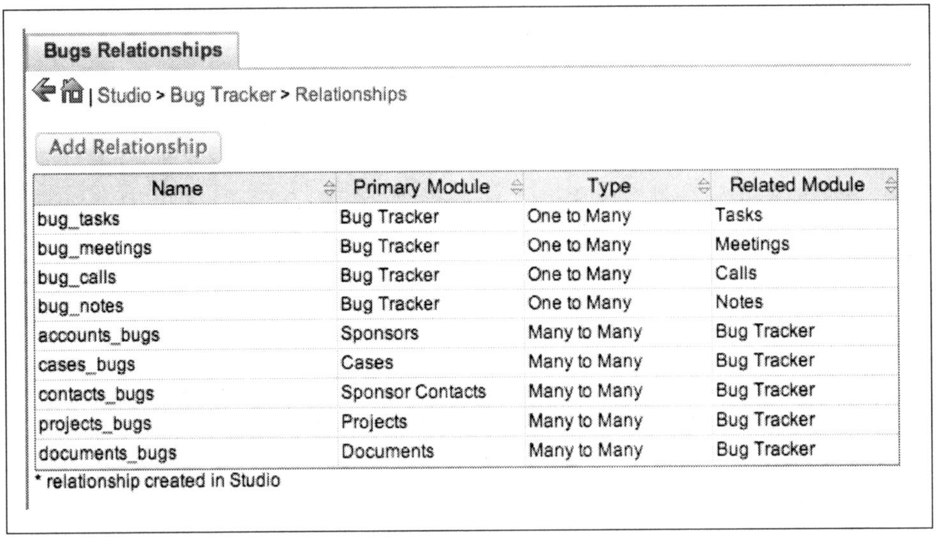

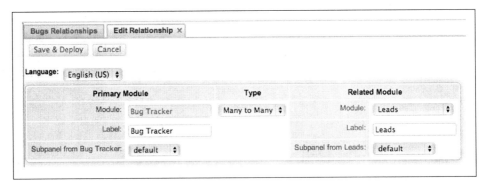

Figure 2-9. List of relationships for a module in Studio

You can double-click on any relationship to see the details of it, and click 'Add Relationship' if you want to add a new relationship. The relationship editor in Studio allows you to add either a One-to-One, One-to-Many, or a Many-to-Many relationship between the current module and another one. You can also specify the label to use to identify the subpanel on the DetailView of a record, as well as specify the subpanel layout to use for the relationship.

Figure 2-10. Editing a Relationship through Studio

When you save the new relationship, it will automatically add the needed UI components to expose the relationship and enable users to control it. This differs depending upon the relationship type used as follows:

- For One-to-One relationships there will be a field on both the primary and related module's EditView for selecting the record to relate to, and a field on each module's DetailView that will display a link to the related record.

- For One-to-Many relationships, there will be a field on both the primary module's EditView for selecting the record to relate to, and a field on the module's DetailView that will display a link to the related record. For the related module, a subpanel will exist on the DetailView for displaying all the related Primary Module records, and you can add and remove records from there.

- For Many-to-Many relationships, on both the primary and related module's DetailView, a subpanel will exist for displaying all the related records from the opposite module, and you can add and remove records from there.

Customizing the language string used in your module

Sometimes, one organization's 'Account' is another's 'Company'. Or maybe you like to refer to a 'Cell Phone' rather than a 'Mobile Phone'. The lexicon for each organization can change based upon how you work, what the entities you work with are, and even what region of the world you are located in. While SugarCRM provides official translations in over 20 languages, and the Sugar community provides translations for over 70 different languages—sometimes the language you use in your business just doesn't match what Sugar provides out of the box. Fortunately, you can change this.

There are many ways to attack this problem:

- If you want to change the label for a field, you can do this in the field properties as we saw earlier in this chapter.

- If you want to change the label for a field in one of the views only, you can click on the edit icon on the field to change it.

- If you are looking for a particular string that's a problem, you can click on the 'Labels' link under the module to see all the defined strings for that module and change it there.

- Dropdown values in a form can be edited using the Dropdown Editor.

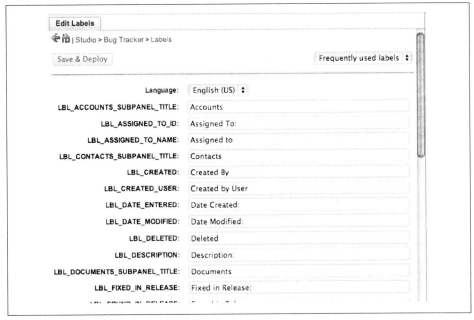

Figure 2-11. Editing labels in Studio

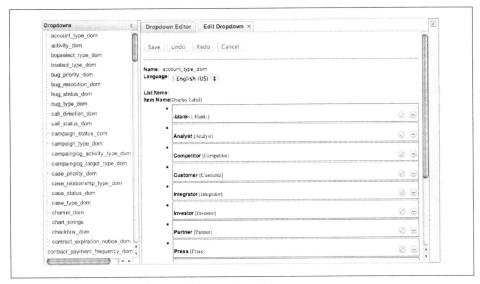

Figure 2-12. Adjusting Dropdowns in the Dropdown Editor

All strings in the product are completely translatable and modifiable, so there's no barrier to changing any label in the application to better suit your organization's needs.

But if we are looking to truly build a custom application for your organization, clearly the built-in modules won't suffice your needs. Fortunately, there is another GUI-based tool for handling this called Module Builder.

Building new modules using Module Builder

Where Studio is the tool for customizing the out-of-the-box modules in SugarCRM, Module Builder is the complimentary tool for building new modules in the product. It uses the same general UI as Studio, even sharing the same tools for adding and editing fields, changing layouts, and building relationships to other modules. The big difference comes in the initial definition of the module and the package, so let's take a look at it.

Defining your new module

In order to build a new module using Module Builder, you first must define a package to contain it. The package is just a container for one or more modules, and it provides a way to have all the modules you want to define for an application pulled together in one cohesive suite. To do this, just go into Module Builder from the Administration area of Sugar, and click on the link 'New Package' to get started.

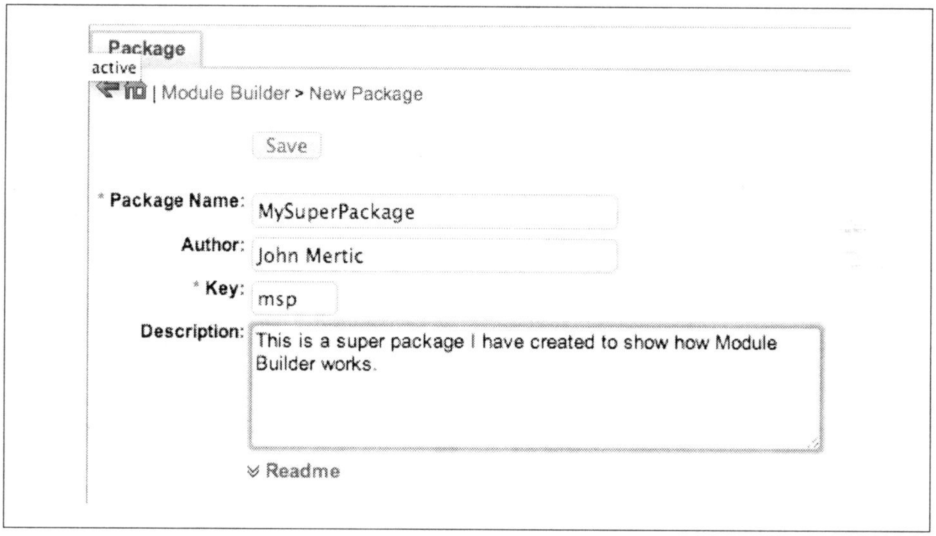

Figure 2-13. Adding a new package through Module Builder

The two important pieces of data here are the Package Name, which identifies your package inside Module Builder and Module Loader, as well as the Key field. The value for the Key field is used as a prefix for the name of your module in the code base, and is a unique identifier for the modules you create in this package (it will be used as a prefix for the module name in the code base), which helps ensure upgrade safeness and protects against a module of the same name coming out and replacing your module. You can also put your name in as the author and drop in a brief description of what the package provides.

Now once you have a package, it's time to add a module to it. Simply click on the 'New Module' link on the subsequent package to bring up a screen for creating a module.

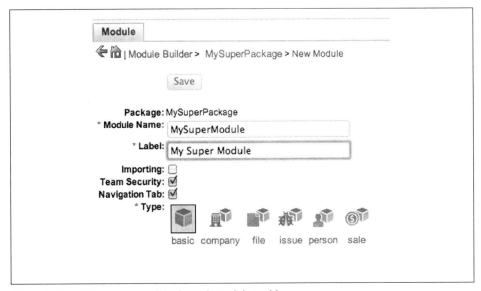

Figure 2-14. Adding a new module through Module Builder

The nice part about building modules in SugarCRM is that you can use the existing templates to help design them faster. So let's say you are building a new module to track people; there's a Person template that brings in all the fields you would normally expect to have when tracking a person, including the ability to import vCards of person data into the module. And this continues into the other available templates of Company, File, Issue, and Sale, which takes away the tediousness of building a new module of a very common type. And rest assured that if the module you are building doesn't fit into one of these molds, the Basic template has the bare-bones list of fields needed so that you can build on to fit in with the goals you are looking to accomplish.

When you click 'Save', you now have a new module ready to work with. The same tools that we showed previously in this chapter with Studio are also available inside Module Builder to add and edit fields, modify layouts, and build new relationships. It's best practice to do all of the customization work for the custom modules you create through Module Builder in Module Builder itself, rather than making these changes in Studio after the fact.

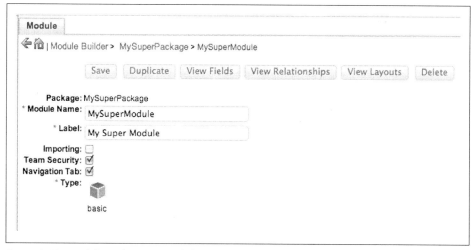

Figure 2-15. Module as shown in Module Builder

Deploying the new package to the world

Once you have this wonderful module built, the next step is to get into an instance to start using it. Here you have several options for what to do:

- Deploy the module to your current instance by clicking 'Deploy'
- Download the package of the file, which can be installed directly on any other SugarCRM instance by clicking 'Publish'
- Export the package as it exists on Module Builder, so that you can continue development on it on another instance by clicking Export

These options give you lots of flexibility in terms of how you want to deploy your package. If it's an add-on you intend to distribute for others to use, then the Publish option makes the most sense. If it's just something for your local Sugar install, then Deploy will install the package right then and there on it. And the Export option gives you a way to back up your custom modules you created.

So you can see that the Module Builder complements Studio in defining the look and feel of a module, and how Sugar Logic comes into place to make layouts more dynamic to suit your needs. But what if you want to truly automate your organization and help reduce data entry and improve communication between the people using the application? This is where Workflow comes into play.

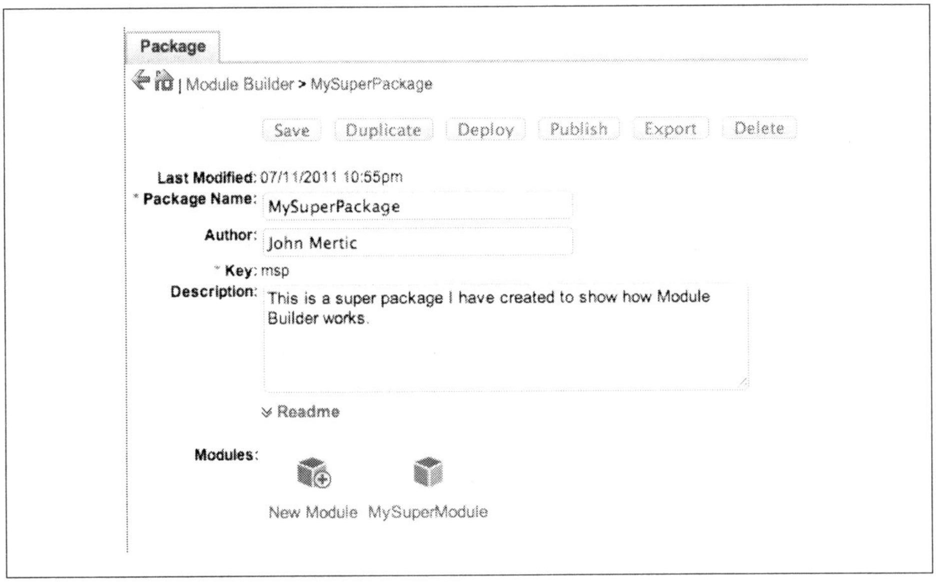

Figure 2-16. Package in Module Builder

Defining Workflows

Workflows enable you to create logic hooks using an easy-to-use user interface instead of having to write PHP code. This is especially useful for those with little or no programming experience; they can simply go through the dialogs to create the logic they wish to add. They leverage the Logic Hooks framework built-in to SugarCRM under the hood, making it easy to build some of the most common business logic scenarios with ease.

The Workflow module is tucked away in the Admin panel under the title 'Workflow Management'. To create your workflow definition, you'll start by clicking the 'Create Workflow Definition' link in the shortcut menu.

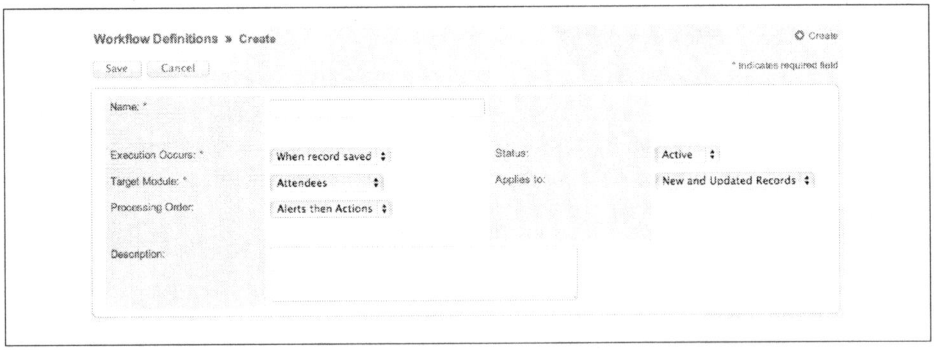

Figure 2-17. Create Workflow Dialog

The definition of a workflow is pretty straightforward. First, you'll need to indicate whether the workflow should be executed when a record is saved or at a specified time interval; the latter lending it to more time-sensitive data changes across all the records in the module and the former for more process-oriented data changes on the current record being saved. You then specify the module the workflow applies to, indicate whether to process alerts or actions first (we'll look at what these are further along in this chapter), and then decide if we should run this workflow against new records, updated records, or both (this option only applies to workflows executed on the save of a record).

Once you click save, you will then be able to define the guts of the workflow: conditions, alerts, and actions. Let's dig into what they are and how to build them.

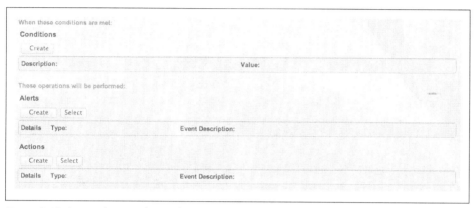

Figure 2-18. Screen showing the conditions, alerts, and actions for a workflow

Create conditions for workflow execution

Conditions for a workflow are simply the set of rules that determine if a workflow should run. It looks at the current state of the record, comparing it with the previous state, based upon the rules you state. These rules are easy to build thanks to a wizard that walks you right through them.

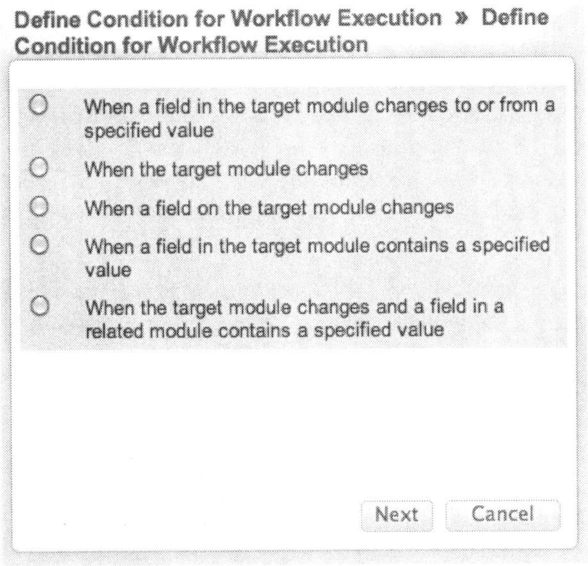

Define Condition for Workflow Execution » Define
Condition for Workflow Execution

○ When a field in the target module changes to or from a
  specified value

○ When the target module changes

○ When a field on the target module changes

○ When a field in the target module contains a specified
  value

○ When the target module changes and a field in a
  related module contains a specified value

Next   Cancel

Figure 2-19. Options for Workflow Conditions

The main options you have are to execute the workflow if:

- Any change happens in the module
- A certain field changes in the module
- A certain field changes to or from a specified value
- A certain field has a specified value
- There is any change in the module when a related field is a specified value

You can add as many conditions as you like to you workflow, which enables you to tightly define exactly when the business logic you wish to execute is called. Let's now learn about what you can do if all of the workflow's conditions are met.

Alerting and Actions for a workflow

Many times, all that needs to happen when fields change or a module changes is that someone needs to know about it. The simplest thing to do when your workflow conditions are met is to send someone an email, which you can define through an Alert action.

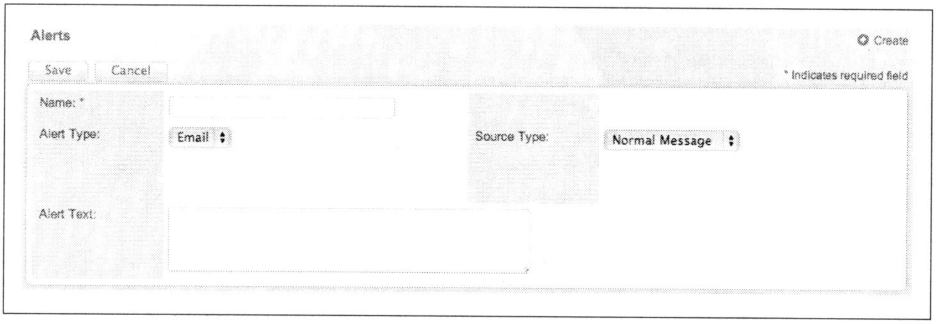

Figure 2-20. Creating a workflow alert

First, you'll want to create the alert definition, which is simply a specification of the email to send. You can keep this simple with a normal text email, or you can define an email template and pull in fields from the affected record and add additional formatting for a more custom email to send out. Once this is defined, you just need to specify the email addresses to send the alert to. There's another wizard for this if you click on 'Create' under the 'Alert Recipient List' subpanel on the Alert's DetailView.

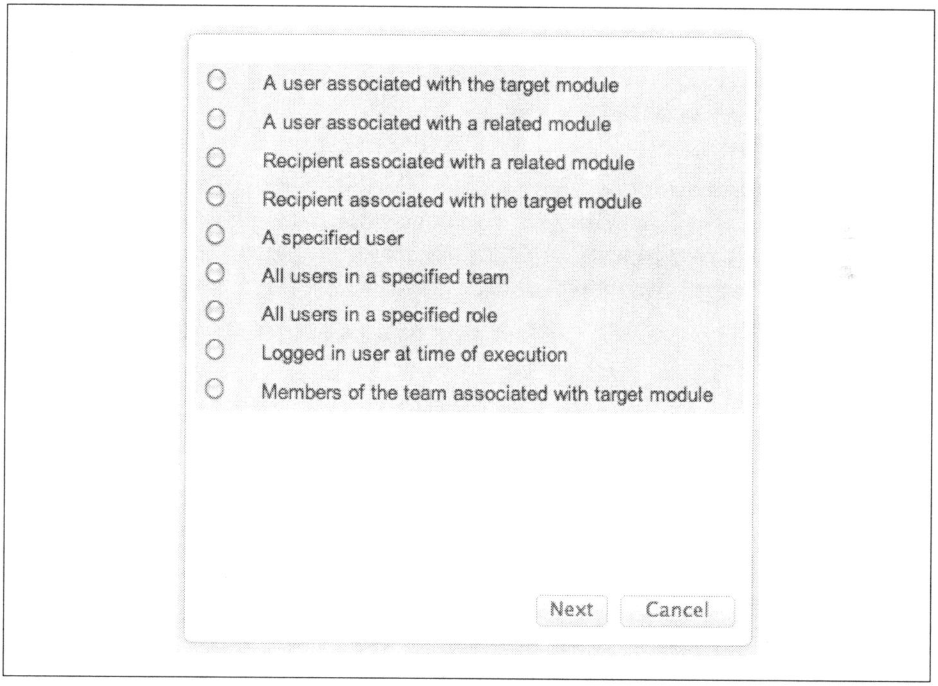

Figure 2-21. Options for selecting a user to send the alert email to

This gives you lots of flexibility in choosing whom to send the alert to, whether being a user derived from the record, a specific user, or just the user who did the action to kick off the workflow.

While letting someone know that something took place, often times that user will just need to go into the system and perform some action as a result of it. Wouldn't it be nice if the workflow just did that for you? It can by defining an action to take place if the conditions of the workflow are met.

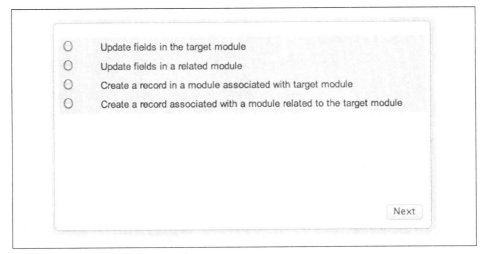

○ Update fields in the target module

○ Update fields in a related module

○ Create a record in a module associated with target module

○ Create a record associated with a module related to the target module

Next

Figure 2-22. Action options in Workflow

The main two options you have here are to update a field in the record or in a related record, or create new record that you can optionally have related to this one. And since you can specify as many actions as you like for a condition, you can have many different fields or record changes based upon a single change in a record.

The actions and alerts make it possible to truly automate your organization using Workflows.

Summary

In this chapter, we looked at the various GUI developer tools SugarCRM has to offer, and what they can do to help us build a custom application for our organization. The tools here take away the need to have a developer make the simple changes to get your application up and running, and speeds up the development time of your application in turn.

Now that we have a great background on the SugarCRM platform as a whole, let's build an application using the tools we just saw and see what we can build without having to touch any code.

CHAPTER 3

Building your application using the Sugar GUI Developer tools

Now is when the fun begins. With a healthy knowledge of the SugarCRM platform, and everything that the SugarCRM developer GUI tools can do, we are now going to dive right into building a sample application on the platform. This application will have many pieces to it, from visual layout to business logic to external services integration. We'll break apart the building of the application over the next several chapters, starting in this chapter with building the core modules and visual layouts. We'll build upon it in the next chapter with business logic and custom forms, and in the final chapter with integrating it out with external services.

So with no further ado, let's dig in to what the application will be and how to design it.

Application overview

For our exercise, we will be building an application to manage a conference. Conferences have concepts very similar to managing customers in terms of how they manage sponsors, but they also have different entities such as attendees and speakers to manage. There's also some additional "glue" modules needed, such as one that can group sponsorships, attendees, and speakers for an entire single event itself. We'll also want to track feedback from attendees, including session feedback, and keep that with the speaker to help decide the schedule for future events.

So overall, we are looking at three major sections to the application:

- *Sponsor management* that has all the details on sponsors, as well as a workflow for recruiting new sponsors and targeting them for sponsorships
- *Attendee management* that records all of the attendees coming to the event
- *Speaker management* that tracks the incoming speaker submissions, helps with sorting through the talk abstracts, and then tracks feedback from attendees about the talk after the fact.

Let's take a look at how to build these modules with Studio and Module Builder

Customizing out-of-the-box modules with Studio

Coming from a developer background, we always want to reinvent the wheel with everything we do. But sometimes a more pragmatic approach is to see what's already built that you can leverage easily. This is why SugarCRM is such a compelling platform to build upon, as many of the main module types an organization may use are already there.

But, just because they are there doesn't mean we don't need to customize them a bit. Let's take a look at doing this for Sponsor management in our conference application.

Sponsors

For this module, we'll use the out-of-the-box Accounts module and its relationship with the Contacts module to track all of the sponsors for the conference itself. The nice part about using these modules is that they come with the built-in relationships to other modules such as Calls, Meetings, and Notes, so we don't have to worry about doing all the linkups between them all. The process for recruiting, managing, and communicating with our sponsors will be the same flow as the typical lead generation and sales automation workflows, so it makes sense to use the existing modules and augment the lexicon used instead of reinventing the modules.

We'll take the same approach for the related Contacts module, renaming it 'Sponsor Contacts' and changing all the Account and Contact verbiage to Sponsor and Sponsor Contact instead.

 If you have access to the source code, do a search against all the *.lang.php* files to find where the string is used. Otherwise, you'll need to go through each module's labels in Studio and the Dropdown Editor to change them all manually.

Sponsorships

To manage sponsorships, we will reuse the existing Opportunities module, changing again the lexicon to match what a sponsorship would be rather than a sales opportunity. The choice to use this existing module instead of building out a custom module just for this purpose is interesting. If you look at how you would manage a sponsorship, it's the same pattern as when you are gauging an opportunity to sell something. It starts off by identifying what the organization is into buying (i.e., what sponsorship they are looking at) and manages them to sale completion (i.e., when they approve the sponsorship). Tracking it this way also allows one to see trends in what sponsorships a

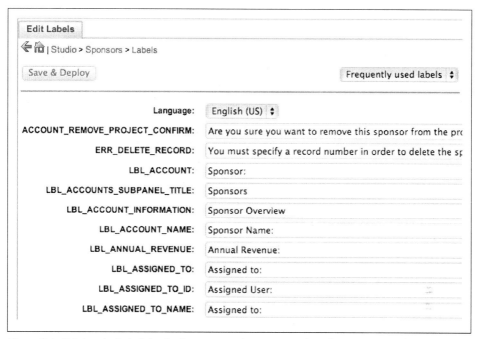

Figure 3-1. Editing the Labels in the Sponsors mode to remove the references to Accounts

sponsor has done in the past versus which ones they were targeted toward doing, giving better insight into selling to sponsors down the road.

We'll need to make a few changes to the module to make it all work out. We need to tread lightly here, since there's all sorts of behind-the-scenes magic that ties into other modules that we don't want to disturb. However, we also want to simplify the data entry process so that when certain options are selected, we can pre-populate fields directly. Sounds like Sugar Logic to the rescue here!

We'll use Sugar Logic to power two fields, 'Sponsorship Name' and 'Amount'. For 'Amount', we'll want to change the 'Opportunity Type' field to 'Level' first, and change the options to match the various sponsorship types we will provide. Then, we will have a bit of Sugar Logic to calculate the 'Amount' field based upon the 'Level' we have chosen.

We are using an ifElse function condition that is nested to pull this off, having a check for each possible value of 'Level'.

When building formulas, the field references reflect the database field name ('$opportunity_type') instead of the field label ('Level').

Figure 3-2. Formula Builder for the amount field

Next comes the 'Sponsorship Name' field, which is what is shown everywhere in the application as the primary field for the module. We don't want people to just enter anything here, but to keep it in a good form that can be easy to read and understand. To do this, we'll also leverage the 'Level' field, here just concatenating it with the string 'Sponsorship' to display in this field.

This automatically updates all the text entry fields in the module as well, so when someone changes it inline, the fields will automatically update as you change the value. It will also process on the backend if some sort of programmatic change to the 'Level' field occurs.

Figure 3-3. Formula Builder for Sponsorship Name field

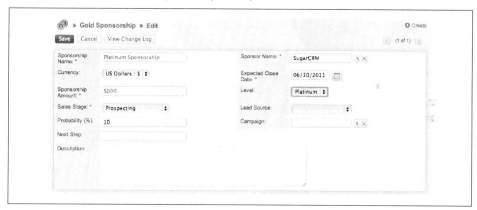

Figure 3-4. EditView for a Sponsorship

 By making the 'Sponsorship Name' and 'Sponsorship Amount' fields calculated, they automatically become read-only on EditViews. You can change this only if you customize the vardef for the field itself, by setting the 'enforced' property to 'false'.

This completes all of the customizations we'll do through Studio for the out-of-the-box modules. Now, let's dig into Module Builder to build out the other new modules we'll use for our conference management application.

New modules to create with Module Builder

There's no such thing as a "one-size-fits-all" CRM application, let alone a business application. Where changing the lexicon and adding a few fields can get you so far with customizing the application to suit your needs, eventually you need to take it to the next step by building additional modules to cover the functionality needed. Back in Chapter 2, we introduced Module Builder, which has the functionality to do just this. This tool will help us build out the final two major pieces of the puzzle—Attendee and Speaker Management—as well as building the needed Events module, which will help us group all of the pieces together.

Attendees

Attendees are just people, and luckily, as we learned back in Chapter 2, Module Builder has just the template for that. So we'll base this module off of the Person template, making one small modification of changing the label of 'Department' to 'Organization' since we won't be adding a related company module for each attendee. We can do these easily by editing the field.

Figure 3-5. Changing the label for the 'Department' field to 'Organization'

Speakers

We're going to be doing a few things to aide speaker management in our module. The goal is to manage the entire call for papers process, as well as managing incoming feedback about the sessions given by the speakers. To pull this off, we'll use three modules: Speakers, Sessions, and Feedback. Let's look at how to build them.

The Speakers module, just like the Attendees module, is based on the Person template, including the same change we made there to have the 'Department' field be 'Organization' instead so we don't have to have a separate Speaker Companies module. We'll also do another label change for the module, this time to have the 'Description' field for the record instead hold the speaker's bio information. We'll also add a relationship to the special 'Activities' module, which allows us to track calls, meetings, tasks, notes, and emails related to them.

The oddball Activities module

You'll see two subpanels in some modules' DetailViews: 'Activities' and 'History'. These are designed by default to work with the built-in Calls, Meetings, Tasks, Notes, and Emails module as a way of grouping together upcoming Activity related to the record, as well as tracking historical touch points made in regards to the records that are logged in SugarCRM. It's a bit different than most related modules, in that it can only be a One-to-many relationship into it, and it drops two subpanels into your module instead of one like other module relationships do. You also don't get a specific field on the Call, Meeting, Note, Task, or Email record for the module, but instead it is added to a flex relate field so that each of those field types can only be related to one other record of any of the valid types at a time.

Next up is the Sessions module, which by default will have a many-to-one relationship with the Speakers module (which is added from the Speakers module end as you can see in Figure 3-6), as well as into the Feedback module we'll build next. We'll base it off the Basic template, since the module is a fairly simple one with only one additional field needing to be added. This field is named 'Status,' which will be a dropdown field that is one of 'Under Review,' 'Accepted,' or 'Declined.'

Name	Primary Module	Type	Related Module
pos_speakers_pos_sessions	Speakers	One to Many	Sessions
pos_speakers_activities	Speakers	One to Many	Activities

Figure 3-6. Speakers module relationships

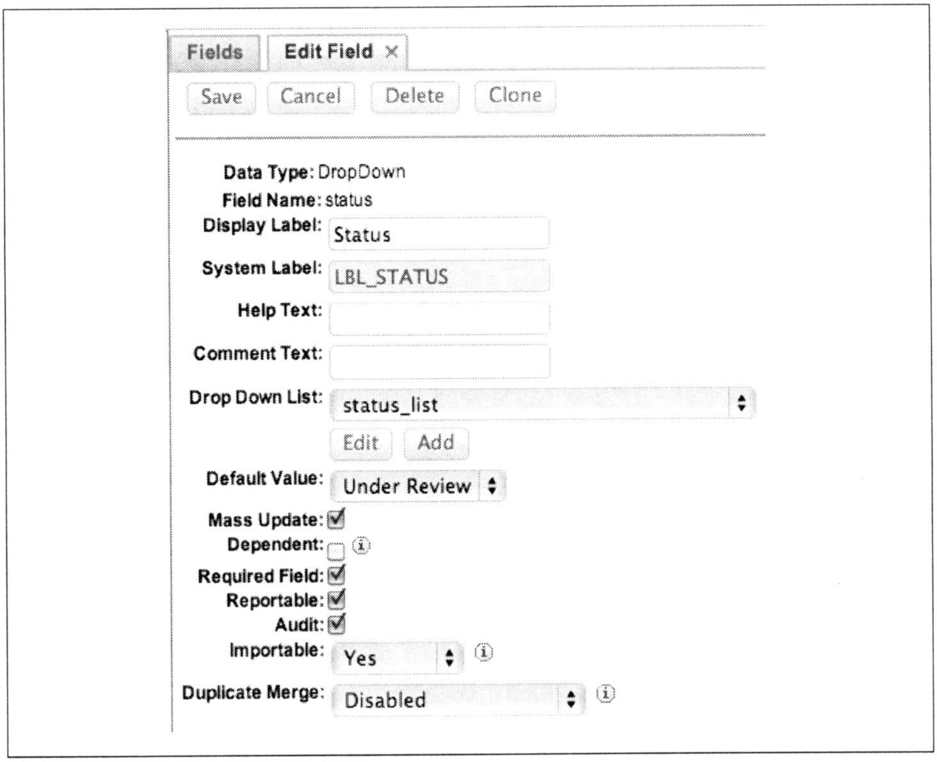

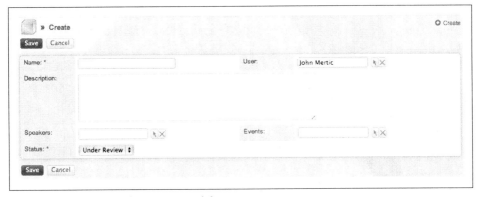

Figure 3-7. Adding field 'Status' to the Sessions module

We'll also add this field to the layouts as well, and rearrange things to include the link to the event (from the Events module we'll look at in the next section).

Figure 3-8. EditView for the Sessions module

Now we'll add the Feedback module, which links back to the Sessions module in a many-to-one relationship. We'll use the basic template for this module as well, but will make three modifications to the fields and layout:

- First off, we'll add a new field, named 'Rating,' which is a set of radio buttons enabling a talk to be rated on a scale of 1 being the lowest and 5 the highest rating. This field will appear in all views.

- Next, we'll change the label of the 'Description' field to be 'Notes' instead, since this is where we are looking for comments from the attendees on the speakers and the session.

- Finally, we are going to be removing the 'Name' field from the layout. This will take a few steps to make happen since this is a primary field for the module, as well as a required one.

To remove the 'Name' field from the layout, we also need to remove the requirement for the field, so all of the forms will save correctly without it being there. But also, we need to provide some sort of value for this field, just like we did before in the Sponsorships module 'Name' field. We'll pull Sugar Logic out of our bag of tricks again here, having it drop in whatever is in the 'Notes' field into the 'Name' field.

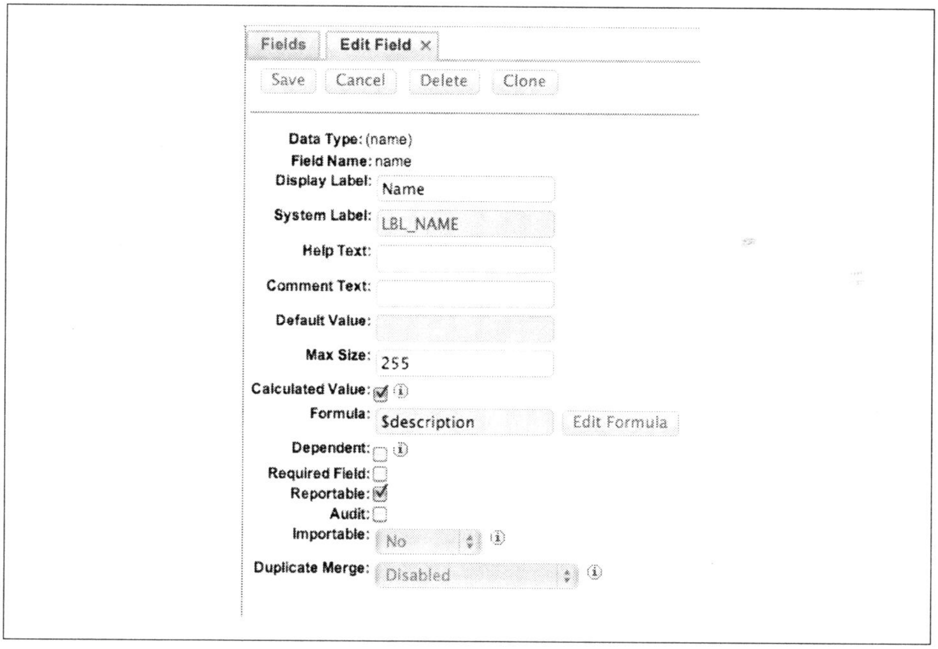

Figure 3-9. Adjusting the 'Name' field in the Feedback module

We've been pretty pedestrian in the customizations in this area, but there's a lot of functionality already in the management of this process with just laying out the module and field relationships. In Chapter 4, we'll really look to add some Logic Hooks and other custom code to help automate the workflow.

Events

The final module, Events, is perhaps the most important one in a sense since it pulls all the other modules together nicely. It also enables us to have a bird's eye view of an event, showing all the sponsorships, attendees, and sessions in one view. It's also important since it enables us to reuse our application for new events, leveraging the existing data and insight from previous ones in make decisions.

We'll base the module off of the Basic template, since really we just need a name and description field for the event itself. The magic comes with relationships; we'll add one-to-many relationships into the Sponsorships and Sessions modules and a many-to-many relationship to the Attendees module. This gives us the ability to capture all the people, events, and organizations involved in the event in one nice view.

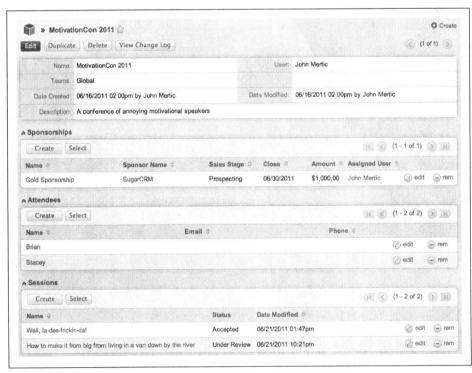

Figure 3-10. Detail View for a sample event

With that, we've built all the modules we'll need for our application.

Summary

In this chapter, we started the process of building a new application for managing conferences using the SugarCRM platform as a basis. We used several of the out-of-the-box modules for some of the work, renaming according to the lexicon that is more appropriate for managing sponsors and sponsorship activities, as these modules had the built-in workflow and pieces in place that made sense to leverage for our application. We then built a few custom modules, based off the already existing templates in Module Builder, to handle managing attendees, speakers, and the overall event. In the process, we saw the power of Studio and Module Builder in creating these modules quickly, as well as using Sugar Logic for doing field calculations to help speed up data entry.

With this design, you could go a long way and implement a very successful conference management application. But if you really want to help optimize the workflow and do some cool things, you'll want to dig below the covers and do some custom PHP coding, leveraging the extensible SugarCRM application framework. We'll see how to do that up next in Chapter 4.

Diving deeper with custom code

So if you've got to this point, you've built out the core of the conference management application. And this core does quite a few things, allowing us to track and manage all of the sponsors, speakers, and attendees for a specific event as well as across various events. If you were developing this core from scratch, it may take you a month or more to get to this point, but with the ease of working with the various SugarCRM GUI developer tools such as Studio and Module Builder, we could pull this off in a few hours and be ready for the stakeholders to start playing with the newly built application right away. This fact alone makes building such an application on the SugarCRM platform a no-brainier, and alleviates all sorts of extra work for you as a developer.

Even with all of that built, there's still more that can be done to better streamline the workflow of the application. It would be great to not only bring information about the data in the system and its changing state, but also to automate common and tedious tasks within the system to make it easier to use. Luckily, SugarCRM has a rich and powerful API for building these sorts of customizations with ease, and in this chapter we'll look at how to do a few of these through easy-to-build custom PHP code.

Bring the new happens with the conference into the Activity Stream

The Activity Stream was a feature added back in Sugar 5.2 that brought social networking inside of your organization, enabling your organization to communicate just like they were using Twitter or Facebook. Having this integrated into SugarCRM gives the added benefit of hooking module activities to it as well so that the application can post when records are added or changed based upon the criteria you provide. This will be especially handy in Chapter 5, where we will be adding new records from forms outside of your application, perhaps from the conference website.

Out of the box, support comes with having these alerts being posted to the Activity Stream for the Contacts, Opportunities, and Leads modules, which immediately enables the Sponsorship management portion of our application to leverage this ability.

Figure 4-1. My Activity Stream dashlet

But what about Speaker and Attendee management? Let's see how we can add some custom code to make this happen.

Show new attendees in the Activity Stream

The first item to tackle is showing when we have new attendee registrations added to the application. This involves adding a short segment of code that registers the logic hook and that will post the update to the Activity Stream. After that, the next task will be to go into the Activity Streams administrator settings and enable the Attendees module to show in the Activity Stream.

To start, let's add the logic hook that will be used to push items into the Activity Stream. The file is named *AttendeeFeed.php*, and it will located in the custom/modules/pos_Attendees/SugarFeeds/ directory.

```php
<?php

require_once('modules/SugarFeed/feedLogicBase.php');

class AttendeeFeed extends FeedLogicBase
{
    public $module = 'pos_Attendees';

    public function pushFeed($bean, $event, $arguments)
    {
        $text = '';
        if(empty($bean->fetched_row)) {
            $text = '[' . $bean->module_dir . ':' . $bean->id . ':' . $bean->name.']
just registered.';
        }

        if(!empty($text)){
```

```
        SugarFeed::pushFeed2($text, $bean);
    }
  }
}
```

The key here is the pushFeed() method, which contains the logic for determining if the record should be pushed into the Activity Stream or not. This method is called on every save of an Attendee record, so the method needs to check if a previous record exists. This is simple to do by checking if an existing record was fetched before the save (and the contents of the record is stored in the $bean->fetched_row array). If it is, we define the string to add in a format that can be parsed as a link in the Activity Stream itself.

To enable the Attendees module in the Activity Stream, simply go to the Admin > Activity Streams panel and checkbox the 'Attendees' option to enable it.

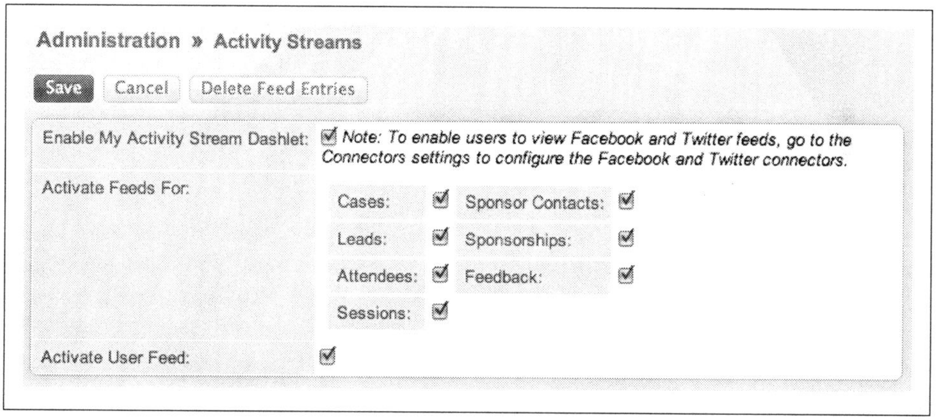

Figure 4-2. Activity Streams administration panel

Now, if a new attendee is saved, a record will be added to the Activity Stream for it.

View incoming speaker proposals in Activity Stream

We can do the same thing for speaker proposals as well. This one here will have a few more options; not only will this push when a new session proposal comes in, but it will also post to the Activity Stream when it's been accepted or rejected.

```php
<?php

require_once('modules/SugarFeed/feedLogicBase.php');

class SessionsFeed extends FeedLogicBase
{
    public $module = 'pos_Sessions';

    public function pushFeed($bean, $event, $arguments)
    {
```

```
        $text = '';
        if(empty($bean->fetched_row)) {
              $text = 'Newly added session abstract [' . $bean->module_dir . ':' .
        $bean->id . ':' . $bean->name.']';
        }
        else {
              if(!empty($bean->fetched_row['status'] )
        && $bean->fetched_row['status'] != $bean->status
        && $bean->status == 'Accepted'){
                    $text = 'Session [' . $bean->module_dir . ':' . $bean->id . ':' .
        $bean->name. '] has been accepted';
              }
              if(!empty($bean->fetched_row['status'] )
        && $bean->fetched_row['status'] != $bean->status
        && $bean->status == 'Declined'){
                    $text = 'Session [' . $bean->module_dir . ':' . $bean->id . ':' .
        $bean->name. '] has been declined';
              }
        }

        if(!empty($text)){
              SugarFeed::pushFeed2($text, $bean);
        }
    }
}
```

So this logic hook has two parts to it. The first check is the same sort of thing done above with the Attendees Activity Stream hook, checking to see if this is a newly added record to the Sessions module and if so then write out to the Activity Stream about the newly created record. If the record is already existing one, the next step is to see if the status has changed to one of the two action values. If it has changed to 'Accepted', then it will write out a message to the Activity Stream that the session has been accepted, and if it has changed to 'Declined', then the message instead will reflect it being declined. We'll then enable the module for Activity Streams just as we did in the Attendees module above.

We'll build upon this example later in this chapter to have additional business logic for changes to Sessions records, automating the notification of speakers of the status of their proposals automatically.

See feedback immediately in Activity Stream.

For users working the system, it can be a pretty encouraging thing to see how attendees feel the conference is going (especially if the feedback is positive). We can do this with the same approach we used in the Attendees module, by making an Activity Stream logic hook to write a message with the feedback that is to be added.

```
<?php

require_once('modules/SugarFeed/feedLogicBase.php');

class FeedbackFeed extends FeedLogicBase
```

```
    {
        public $module = 'pos_Feedback';

        public function pushFeed($bean, $event, $arguments)
        {
            $text = '';
            if(empty($bean->fetched_row)) {
                $text = 'New feedback added ( rating: ' . $bean->rating . ' ): ' .
    $bean->description.'';
            }

            if(!empty($text)){
                SugarFeed::pushFeed2($text, $bean);
            }

        }
    }
```

The message to be written to the Activity Stream will have the rating the attendee gave, along with any feedback they have provided as a part of their review. This will become an even more useful tool in Chapter 5 when we build an external form that attendees can post their feedback to that will automatically add it to our application and put an entry in the Activity Stream for it.

Figure 4-3. Activity Stream with entries from the Feedback and Sessions modules

With that, we have more fully integrated all of the modules in our application into the Activity Streams, which has given users of the system a more realtime view of the changes happening to records in the system. Let's now see how we can use the same logic hook technique to automate a common task in this application: speaker proposal acceptance and rejection.

Automate speaker acceptance and rejection

A common task in conference management is accepting and rejecting talks proposed by the various speakers. This involves reviewing the proposals sent in, making decisions on whether to accept or reject them, and then notifying the speakers either way on the decision. While SugarCRM cannot take away the human decision element of this process, it can automate the notification process. Let's see how:

```php
<?php
// Do not store anything in this file that is not part of the array or the hook
//version.  This file will be automatically rebuilt in the future.
 $hook_version = 1;
$hook_array = Array();
// position, file, function
$hook_array['before_save'] = Array();
$hook_array['before_save'][] = Array(1, 'pos_Sessions push feed',
'custom/modules/pos_Sessions/SugarFeeds/SessionsFeed.php','SessionsFeed', 'pushFeed');
$hook_array['before_save'][] = Array(1,
'Session Accepted Hook', 'custom/modules/pos_Sessions/NotifySpeakerHook.php',
'NotifySpeakerHook', 'sendAcceptEmail');
$hook_array['before_save'][] = Array(2,
'Session Declined Hook', 'custom/modules/pos_Sessions/NotifySpeakerHook.php',
'NotifySpeakerHook', 'sendDeclineEmail');



?>
```

First off, we'll need to add to the *existing logic_hooks.php* file in the custom/modules/ pos_Sessions/ directory, adding two entries for before_save logic hooks to send out these emails.

For the hook itself, we'll add a new class named NotifySpeakerHook, which will be defined in the file *custom/modules/pos_Sessions/NotifySpeakerHook.php*.

```php
<?php

class NotifySpeakerHook
{
    public function sendAcceptEmail(SugarBean $bean, $event, $arguments)
    {
        if (!empty($bean->fetched_row['status'] )
&& $bean->fetched_row['status'] != $bean->status
&& $bean->status == 'Accepted'){
            $this->sendEmail($bean,
                'Your proposal has been accepted!',
                "Congratulations, your proposal entitled '{$bean->name} for the".
                        "conference has been accepted."
                );
```

```
        }
    }

    public function sendDeclineEmail(SugarBean $bean, $event, $arguments)
    {
        if(!empty($bean->fetched_row['status'] )
&& $bean->fetched_row['status'] != $bean->status
&& $bean->status == 'Declined'){
            $this->sendEmail($bean,
                'Your proposal has not been accepted',
                "We are sorry to inform you that your proposal entitled".
                            "{$bean->name} has not been accepted for the conference."
                );
        }
    }

    protected function sendEmail(SugarBean $bean, $emailSubject, $emailBody)
    {
        $emailObj = new Email();
        $defaults = $emailObj->getSystemDefaultEmail();
        $mail = new SugarPHPMailer();
        $mail->setMailerForSystem();
        //$mail->IsHTML(true);
        $mail->From = $defaults['email'];
        $mail->FromName = $defaults['name'];
        $mail->ClearAllRecipients();
        $mail->ClearReplyTos();
        $mail->Subject=from_html($emailSubject);
        $mail->Body=from_html($emailBody);
        $mail->prepForOutbound();

        $speaker = new pos_Speakers;
        $speaker->retrieve($bean->pos_speake680dpeakers_ida);
        if ( !empty($speaker->id) && !empty($speaker->email1) ) {
            $mail->AddAddress($speaker->email1);
        }

        //now create email
        if (@$mail->Send()) {
            $emailObj->to_addrs= '';
            $emailObj->type= 'archived';
            $emailObj->deleted = '0';
            $emailObj->name = $mail->Subject ;
            $emailObj->description = $mail->Body;
            $emailObj->description_html = null;
            $emailObj->from_addr = $mail->From;
            $emailObj->parent_type = $speaker->module_dir;
            $emailObj->parent_id = $speaker->id;
            $emailObj->date_sent = TimeDate::getInstance()->nowDb();
            $emailObj->modified_user_id = '1';
            $emailObj->created_by = '1';
            $emailObj->team_id = '1';
            $emailObj->status = 'sent';
            $emailObj->save();
        }
```

```
        }
    }
```

There are two hook functions for sending either the acceptance or rejection email based upon whether the status has changed to 'Accepted' or 'Declined'. Both of these methods level an internal class method named 'sendEmail()', which handles sending the actual email out to the speaker who sent in the session abstract. One thing we do in this process is create an archived email in the application underneath the speaker record. This gives us a record of the email being successfully being sent out to the Speaker.

Calculating Average Session Feedback Score

One quick piece of information people will look for when checking out a session is what the feedback is. While they could page through all of the feedback records to see what the ratings are, it would be much easier to have a quick snapshot summary of the feedback. This functionality is often known as "Roll-ups". While SugarCRM doesn't have a way to do this out of the box or through the developer tools, we can build this functionality into our application very easily. There are two parts to doing this.

```php
<?php

require_once('include/MVC/View/views/view.detail.php');

class pos_SessionsViewDetail extends ViewDetail
{
    /**
     * @see SugarView::display()
     */
    public function display()
    {
        $feedbackCount = 0;
        $feedbackTotal = 0;

        $feedbacks = $this->bean->get_linked_beans('pos_sessions_pos_feedback',
'pos_Feedback');
        foreach($feedbacks as $feedback) {
            $feedbackTotal += (int) $feedback->rating;
            ++$feedbackCount;
        }

        $this->ss->assign("AVERAGE_RATING", round($feedbackTotal/$feedbackCount,1));

        parent::display();
    }
}
```

First off, we need to override the default DetailView code to do this calculation. The SugarBean API has built-in methods for grabbing all of the related records to the current record (get_linked_beans()), which gives us a back an array of Feedback module beans that are related to the given Session record. From there, we simply total up the ratings column, divide it by the total number of Feedback records we come across, and store that as the value for the average rating.

We'll also want to add this field to the detailviewdefs for this module, next to the Status field. To do this, just add an extra entry to the file, setting the 'customCode' attribute to the value calculated in the field view code above.

```php
<?php

$module_name = 'pos_Sessions';
$viewdefs [$module_name] =
array (
  'DetailView' =>
  array (
    'templateMeta' =>
    array (
      'form' =>
      array (
        'buttons' =>
        array (
          0 => 'EDIT',
          1 => 'DUPLICATE',
          2 => 'DELETE',
        ),
      ),
      'maxColumns' => '2',
      'widths' =>
      array (
        0 =>
        array (
          'label' => '10',
          'field' => '30',
        ),
        1 =>
        array (
          'label' => '10',
          'field' => '30',
        ),
      ),
      'useTabs' => false,
      'syncDetailEditViews' => false,
    ),
    'panels' =>
    array (
      'default' =>
      array (
        0 =>
        array (
          0 =>
          array (
            'name' => 'name',
            'label' => 'LBL_NAME',
          ),
          1 =>
          array (
```

```
        'name' => 'assigned_user_name',
        'label' => 'LBL_ASSIGNED_TO_NAME',
      ),
    ),
    1 =>
    array (
      0 =>
      array (
        'name' => 'date_entered',
        'customCode' => '{$fields.date_entered.value} {$APP.LBL_BY}'.\n.'
{$fields.created_by_name.value}',
        'label' => 'LBL_DATE_ENTERED',
      ),
      1 =>
      array (
        'name' => 'date_modified',
        'customCode' => '{$fields.date_modified.value} {$APP.LBL_BY}.\n.'
{$fields.modified_by_name.value}',
        'label' => 'LBL_DATE_MODIFIED',
      ),
    ),
    2 =>
    array (
      0 =>
      array (
        'name' => 'description',
        'comment' => 'Full text of the note',
        'label' => 'LBL_DESCRIPTION',
      ),
    ),
    3 =>
    array (
      0 =>
      array (
        'name' => 'pos_speaker_sessions_name',
      ),
      1 =>
      array (
        'name' => 'pos_events__sessions_name',
      ),
    ),
    4 =>
    array (
      0 =>
      array (
        'name' => 'status',
        'studio' => 'visible',
        'label' => 'LBL_STATUS',
      ),
      1 =>
      array (
        'name' => 'status',
        'studio' => 'visible',
        'label' => 'Average Rating',
        'customCode' => '{$AVERAGE_RATING}',
```

```
            ),
          ),
        ),
      ),
    ),
  );
```

You'll need to do a 'Quick Rebuild and Repair' from the Administration > Repair screen to have this take effect, but when it does, you'll have the Average Rating calculated on the fly each time the DetailView is pulled up.

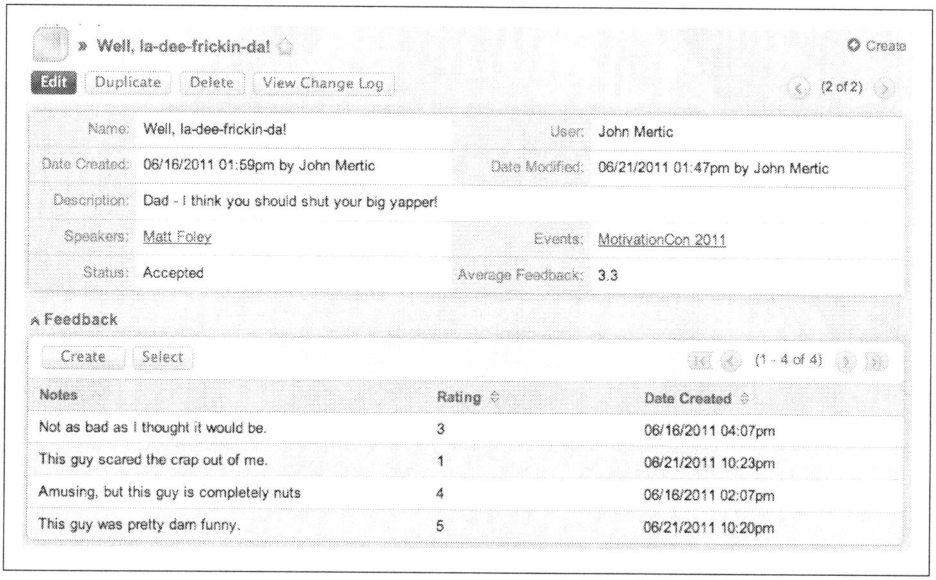

Figure 4-4. Session DetailView with the Average Rating calculated.

Summary

In this chapter, we saw how logic hooks can be used to help automate the workflow of the application to provide increased visibility of events happening in the system. Increased visibility was achieved through incorporating our custom modules with Activity Streams, letting users see what is happening in the application in realtime. We also saw how to automate the speaker notification process through logic hooks that can send out emails when the status changes. Finally, we saw how to modify the display of the Sessions DetailView to provide a roll-up of the feedback for it, giving a calculated average rating based upon the feedback given for the record.

Now that we saw how easy it is to interject custom PHP code into the application, let's now build upon this with seeing how to integrate external applications into this one through Web Services.

CHAPTER 5

Integrating your application with the outside world

Up to this point, all of the customizations done have been inside the SugarCRM application itself. With this we have built a nice workflow inside the application, and streamlined many activities that before would require many data entry points to make the app easier to use and to cut down on data entry errors. But with an application like this, there are more users than just the ones who will log in into the SugarCRM instance. These users are the ones from the outside world who are submitting data we will be importing into the application.

Since the very early days, SugarCRM has had a web services API that used SOAP for interacting with your Sugar instance, and it's one we've used extensively in the third-party integrations that exist in the commercial editions of the product (such as the Office and Lotus Notes plug-ins; iOS, Android, and Blackberry mobile clients; and the self-service portal). In Sugar 5.5, we greatly enhanced the API by simplifying the API calls, added versioning to help avoid API breakages between versions, and implemented REST support in addition to our already existing SOAP support.

Learning more about SugarCRM Web Services API

There's lots of great documentation on these topics on the web. Here are some links to a few great articles:

- Being RESTful with SugarCRM (*http://www.ibm.com/developerworks/library/x-sugarcrmrest/index.html*) talks about interacting with SugarCRM over REST
- Extend SugarCRM REST Web Services to use XML (*http://www.ibm.com/developerworks/opensource/library/x-sugarcrmwebsrv/?ca=drs-*) talks about how to extend the Web Services API to add your own methods and functionality.
- The Sugar Developer Blog Web Services category (*http://developers.sugarcrm.com/wordpress/category/webservices/*) has many articles about using the Web Services API with various different languages.

There are also two client-specific libraries that make it much easier to work with our Web Services API in way that makes it feel closer to working in the native language.

- For Ruby, check out *https://github.com/chicks/sugarcrm*
- For Python, check out *https://github.com/sugarcrm/python_webservices_library*

For our application, there are three different places where external users will interact with our website:

- When Attendees wish to register for the conference
- When prospective speakers want to send in their submissions
- When Attendees wish to give feedback on the sessions they attended.

Let's take a look at each case and how we can leverage SugarCRM Web Services to solve the problem.

Attendee registration form

The first point of contact is for someone to come to your website wanting to attend the conference. For this, we'll want to have a simple-to-use form for them to put in their name and contact information.

Figure 5-1. Attendee Registration Form

On form submission, we will use the SugarCRM Web Services to take the data POSTed from the form and input it into a new Attendee record. Let's check out the code.

```php
<?php

// specify the REST web service to interact with
$url = 'http://localhost/~jmertic/ebook/service/v4/rest.php';

// Open a curl session for making the call
$curl = curl_init($url);

// Tell curl to use HTTP POST
curl_setopt($curl, CURLOPT_POST, true);

// Tell curl not to return headers, but do return the response
curl_setopt($curl, CURLOPT_HEADER, false);
curl_setopt($curl, CURLOPT_RETURNTRANSFER, true);

// Set the POST arguments to pass to the Sugar server
$parameters = array(
    'user_auth' => array(
        'user_name' => 'myuser',
        'password' => md5('mypass'),
        ),
    );
$json = json_encode($parameters);
$postArgs = array(
                'method' => 'login',
                'input_type' => 'JSON',
                'response_type' => 'JSON',
                'rest_data' => $json
                );
curl_setopt($curl, CURLOPT_POSTFIELDS, $postArgs);

// Make the REST call, returning the result
$response = curl_exec($curl);

// Make the REST call, returning the result
$response = curl_exec($curl);
if (!$response) {
    die("Connection Failure.\n");
}

// Convert the result from JSON format to a PHP array
$result = json_decode($response);
if ( !is_object($result) ) {
    var_dump($response);
    die("Error handling result.\n");
}
if ( !isset($result->id) ) {
    die("Error: {$result->name} - {$result->description}\n.");
}

// Get the session id
$sessionId = $result->id;
```

The first part of the code will initialize the Curl object and log in to the SugarCRM instance. Curl is simply a library used in PHP for making HTTP requests to web servers, which is the ideal library to use when working with REST-based web services. Since the data coming back is going to be pure JSON content, we'll want to make sure we only get the actual response body back and ignore the response headers. We then call the 'login' method, which authenticates the given user against the SugarCRM instance. Once we do this, the 'login' method gives us back a session ID, which we will pass to all methods called after this,

Now let's see how to submit the form data into the SugarCRM instance:

```php
// Add registered attendee
$parameters = array(
    'session' => $sessionId,
    'module' => 'pos_Attendees',
    'name_value_list' => array(
        array('name' => 'first_name', 'value' => $_REQUEST['first_name']),
        array('name' => 'last_name', 'value' => $_REQUEST['last_name']),
        array('name' => 'suffix', 'value' => $_REQUEST['suffix']),
        array('name' => 'salutation', 'value' => $_REQUEST['salutation']),
        array('name' => 'title', 'value' => $_REQUEST['title']),
        array('name' => 'department', 'value' => $_REQUEST['organization']),
        array('name' => 'phone_work', '
value' => "({$_REQUEST['area_code']}) {$_REQUEST['phone1']}-{$_REQUEST['phone2']}"),
        array('name' => 'department', 'value' => $_REQUEST['organization']),
        array('name' => 'email1', '
value' => $_REQUEST['email']),
        array('name' => 'primary_address_street', 'value' => $_REQUEST['address']),
        array('name' => 'primary_address_city', 'value' => $_REQUEST['city']),
        array('name' => 'primary_address_state', 'value' => $_REQUEST['state']),
        array('name' => 'primary_address_postalcode', 'value' => $_REQUEST['postal_code']),
        array('name' => 'primary_address_country', 'value' => $_REQUEST['country']),
        array('name' => 'description', 'value' => $_REQUEST['bio']),
        ),
    );
$json = json_encode($parameters);
$postArgs = array(
                'method' => 'set_entry',
                'input_type' => 'JSON',
                'response_type' => 'JSON',
                'rest_data' => $json
                );
curl_setopt($curl, CURLOPT_POSTFIELDS, $postArgs);

// Make the REST call, returning the result
$response = curl_exec($curl);
if (!$response) {
    die("Connection Failure.\n");
}

// Convert the result from JSON format to a PHP array
$result = json_decode($response);
if ( !is_object($result) ) {
    die("Error handling result.\n");
```

```
    }
    if ( !isset($result->id) ) {
        die("Error: {$result->name} - {$result->description}\n.");
    }

    header('Location: registered.html');
```

We'll use the method 'set_entry', which takes the POSTed form data and associates it with the correct fields used in our Attendees module. Upon success, the newly created record ID will be return to us, and we will redirect to a landing page that indicates that the form was submitted successfully. This additional form could have information on how to send in payment, perhaps integrating with a service such as PayPal to enable online payment as a part of the process.

Call for Papers submission form

The next task is to enable prospective speakers to send in their abstracts and bios for inclusion into the program. The form itself is a simple one, just like the one in the previous example, asking for name and contact information, their bio, and talk abstract.

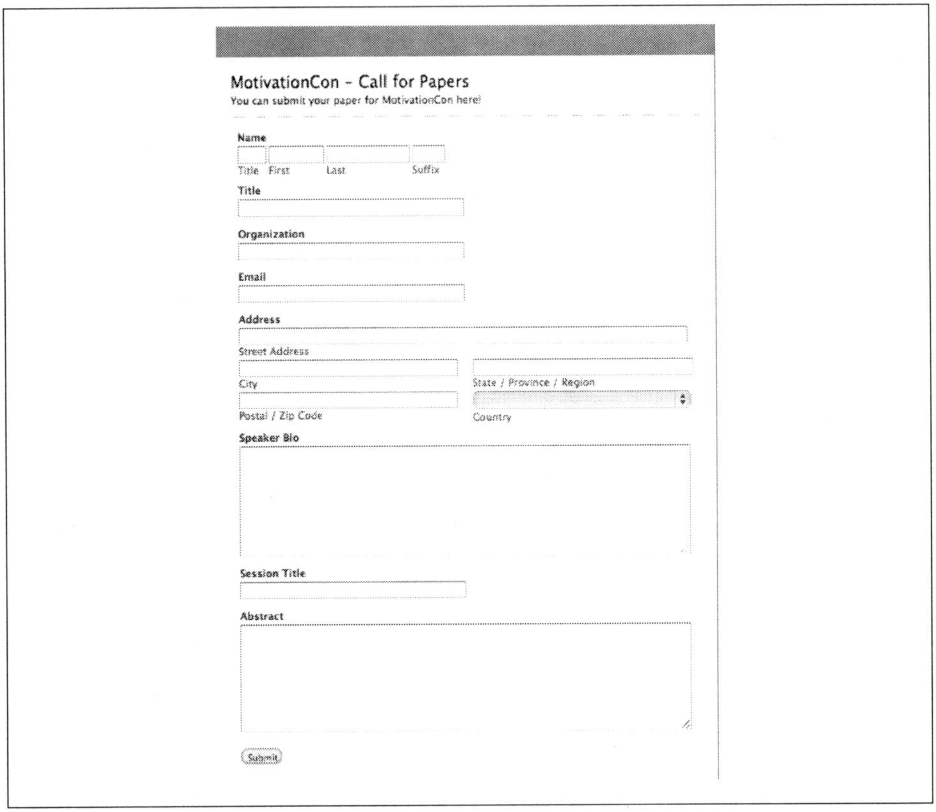

Figure 5-2. Call for Paper submission form

The backend script to handle this is very similar to the one used for Attendee registration, but with a small twist. Let's dig in to it.

```php
<?php

// specify the REST web service to interact with
$url = 'http://localhost/~jmertic/ebook/service/v4/rest.php';

// Open a curl session for making the call
$curl = curl_init($url);

// Tell curl to use HTTP POST
curl_setopt($curl, CURLOPT_POST, true);

// Tell curl not to return headers, but do return the response
curl_setopt($curl, CURLOPT_HEADER, false);
curl_setopt($curl, CURLOPT_RETURNTRANSFER, true);

// Set the POST arguments to pass to the Sugar server
$parameters = array(
    'user_auth' => array(
```

```
              'user_name' => 'myuser',
              'password' => md5('mypassword'),
          ),
      );
$json = json_encode($parameters);
$postArgs = array(
              'method' => 'login',
              'input_type' => 'JSON',
              'response_type' => 'JSON',
              'rest_data' => $json
              );
curl_setopt($curl, CURLOPT_POSTFIELDS, $postArgs);

// Make the REST call, returning the result
$response = curl_exec($curl);

// Make the REST call, returning the result
$response = curl_exec($curl);
if (!$response) {
    die("Connection Failure.\n");
}

// Convert the result from JSON format to a PHP array
$result = json_decode($response);
if ( !is_object($result) ) {
    var_dump($response);
    die("Error handling result.\n");
}
if ( !isset($result->id) ) {
    die("Error: {$result->name} - {$result->description}\n.");
}

// Get the session id
$sessionId = $result->id;
```

First off, we repeat the same login logic from before, grabbing the session ID to use throughout the script. Since speakers can submit in multiple abstracts, we need to check the submitted speaker submission to see if the speaker already exists in the system. For this, we'll assume a speaker with the same name and organization name as one already existing in the system is one we can match against. We'll use the 'get_entry_list' method call for this, which allows us to query against all records in a module.

```
// First, see if the Speaker has submitted before
// Retrieve the contact record we just created
$parameters = array(
    'session' => $sessionId,
    'module_name' => 'pos_Speakers',
    'query' => "pos_speakers.first_name = '{$_POST['first_name']}'".\n"
and pos_speakers.last_name = '{$_POST['last_name']}' ".\n"
and pos_speakers.department = '{$_POST['organization']}'",
    'order_by' => 'last_name',
    'offset' => '',
    'select_fields' => array('first_name','last_name'),
    'link_name_to_fields_array' => array(),
    );
```

```
$json = json_encode($parameters);
$postArgs = array(
                  'method' => 'get_entry_list',
                  'input_type' => 'JSON',
                  'response_type' => 'JSON',
                  'rest_data' => $json
                  );
curl_setopt($curl, CURLOPT_POSTFIELDS, $postArgs);

// Make the REST call, returning the result
$response = curl_exec($curl);
if (!$response) {
    die("Connection Failure.\n");
}

// Convert the result from JSON format to a PHP array
$result = json_decode($response);
if ( !is_object($result) ) {
    var_dump($response);
    die("Error handling result.\n");
}
if ( !isset($result->result_count) ) {
    die("Error: {$result->name} - {$result->description}\n.");
}
```

Now we need to do the appropriate action based upon whether the Speaker was found in the SugarCRM instance or not. If we've found a speaker, we can just use the given speaker ID for the rest of the script. Otherwise, we'll need to add a new speaker record into the SugarCRM instance, and grab the returned ID to use for the next part of the script.

```
if ( $result->result_count > 0 ) {
    // we found them!
    $speakerId = $result->entry_list[0]->id;
}
else {
    // not found, add a new record
    $parameters = array(
        'session' => $sessionId,
        'module' => 'pos_Speakers',
        'name_value_list' => array(
            array('name' => 'first_name', 'value' => $_REQUEST['first_name']),
            array('name' => 'last_name', 'value' => $_REQUEST['last_name']),
            array('name' => 'suffix', 'value' => $_REQUEST['suffix']),
            array('name' => 'salutation', 'value' => $_REQUEST['salutation']),
            array('name' => 'title', 'value' => $_REQUEST['title']),
            array('name' => 'department', 'value' => $_REQUEST['organization']),
            array('name' => 'email1', 'value' => $_REQUEST['email']),
            array('name' => 'primary_address_street', 'value' => $_REQUEST['address']),
            array('name' => 'primary_address_city', 'value' => $_REQUEST['city']),
            array('name' => 'primary_address_state', 'value' => $_REQUEST['state']),
            array('name' => 'primary_address_postalcode',
  'value' => $_REQUEST['postal_code']),
            array('name' => 'primary_address_country',
```

```
  'value' => $_REQUEST['country']),
            array('name' => 'description', 'value' => $_REQUEST['bio']),
            ),
        );
    $json = json_encode($parameters);
    $postArgs = array(
                    'method' => 'set_entry',
                    'input_type' => 'JSON',
                    'response_type' => 'JSON',
                    'rest_data' => $json
                    );
    curl_setopt($curl, CURLOPT_POSTFIELDS, $postArgs);

    // Make the REST call, returning the result
    $response = curl_exec($curl);
    if (!$response) {
        die("Connection Failure.\n");
    }

    // Convert the result from JSON format to a PHP array
    $result = json_decode($response);
    if ( !is_object($result) ) {
        var_dump($response);
        die("Error handling result.\n");
    }
    if ( !isset($result->id) ) {
        die("Error: {$result->name} - {$result->description}\n.");
    }
    $speakerId = $result->id;
}
```

Now that we have a speaker record, let's add in the Session record for the abstract they are submitting to us. Again, we'll simply take the POSTed form data and create the record, grabbing the ID for the newly created record.

```
// Now, let's add a new Session record
$parameters = array(
    'session' => $sessionId,
    'module' => 'pos_Sessions',
    'name_value_list' => array(
        array('name' => 'name', 'value' => $_REQUEST['session_title']),
        array('name' => 'description', 'value' => $_REQUEST['abstract']),
        ),
    );
$json = json_encode($parameters);
$postArgs = array(
                'method' => 'set_entry',
                'input_type' => 'JSON',
                'response_type' => 'JSON',
                'rest_data' => $json
                );
curl_setopt($curl, CURLOPT_POSTFIELDS, $postArgs);

// Make the REST call, returning the result
$response = curl_exec($curl);
```

```
if (!$response) {
    die("Connection Failure.\n");
}

// Convert the result from JSON format to a PHP array
$result = json_decode($response);
if ( !is_object($result) ) {
    var_dump($response);
    die("Error handling result.\n");
}
if ( !isset($result->id) ) {
    die("Error: {$result->name} - {$result->description}\n.");
}

// Get the newly created record id
$talkId = $result->id;
```

Finally, we'll relate the speaker record, which we found or created in the first part of the script, to the session record we created in the second part of the script using the IDs returned back to us from the SugarCRM instance. We'll use the method 'set_relationship' for this, which takes the parent module and record id and lets us specify a record to be related to it based upon a defined relationship.

```
// Now relate the speaker to the session
// Now let's relate the records together
$parameters = array(
    'session' => $sessionId,
    'module_name' => 'pos_Speakers',
    'module_id' => $speakerId,
    'link_field_name' => 'pos_speakers_pos_sessions',
    'related_ids' => array($talkId),
    );
$json = json_encode($parameters);
$postArgs = array(
                'method' => 'set_relationship',
                'input_type' => 'JSON',
                'response_type' => 'JSON',
                'rest_data' => $json
                );
curl_setopt($curl, CURLOPT_POSTFIELDS, $postArgs);

// Make the REST call, returning the result
$response = curl_exec($curl);
if (!$response) {
    die("Connection Failure.\n");
}

// Convert the result from JSON format to a PHP array
$result = json_decode($response);
if ( !is_object($result) ) {
    var_dump($response);
    die("Error handling result.\n");
}

header('Location: submitted.html');
```

After all of this, if the steps are executed successfully, we'll redirect the user to landing page indicating that the save was successful. And on the SugarCRM side of things, you'll have the new session added that is related to the given speaker correctly.

Session Feedback Form

The final piece of the external user integration puzzle is to allow them to post feedback on the sessions they have attended. This is an important thing for conference organizers, as it helps them evaluate how the sessions went and how to better select sessions for next time around.

We'll use a bit of PHP code in the actual feedback form to grab the available sessions to rate, as shown in the code snippet below.

```php
<?php
// Grab the list of sessions for the dropdown


// specify the REST web service to interact with
$url = 'http://localhost/~jmertic/ebook/service/v4/rest.php';

// Open a curl session for making the call
$curl = curl_init($url);

// Tell curl to use HTTP POST
curl_setopt($curl, CURLOPT_POST, true);

// Tell curl not to return headers, but do return the response
curl_setopt($curl, CURLOPT_HEADER, false);
curl_setopt($curl, CURLOPT_RETURNTRANSFER, true);

// Set the POST arguments to pass to the Sugar server
$parameters = array(
    'user_auth' => array(
        'user_name' => 'myuser',
        'password' => md5('mypass'),
        ),
    );
$json = json_encode($parameters);
$postArgs = array(
            'method' => 'login',
            'input_type' => 'JSON',
            'response_type' => 'JSON',
            'rest_data' => $json
            );
curl_setopt($curl, CURLOPT_POSTFIELDS, $postArgs);

// Make the REST call, returning the result
$response = curl_exec($curl);

// Make the REST call, returning the result
$response = curl_exec($curl);
if (!$response) {
```

```
            die("Connection Failure.\n");
    }

    // Convert the result from JSON format to a PHP array
    $result = json_decode($response);
    if ( !is_object($result) ) {
        var_dump($response);
        die("Error handling result.\n");
    }
    if ( !isset($result->id) ) {
        die("Error: {$result->name} - {$result->description}\n.");
    }

    // Get the session id
    $sessionId = $result->id;
```

Again, the usual login code will be done to start things off, giving us back the session ID to use in the subsequent call. Next, we will call the 'get_entry_list' method again to grab a list of sessions available for feedback. Sessions that are available will be ones that were marked as Accepted.

```
    // Retieve the sessions that are available to provide feedback for
    $parameters = array(
        'session' => $sessionId,
        'module_name' => 'pos_Sessions',
        'query' => "pos_sessions.status = 'Accepted'",
        'order_by' => 'name',
        'offset' => '',
        'select_fields' => array('name'),
        'link_name_to_fields_array' => array(),
        );

    $json = json_encode($parameters);
    $postArgs = array(
                    'method' => 'get_entry_list',
                    'input_type' => 'JSON',
                    'response_type' => 'JSON',
                    'rest_data' => $json
                    );
    curl_setopt($curl, CURLOPT_POSTFIELDS, $postArgs);

    // Make the REST call, returning the result
    $response = curl_exec($curl);
    if (!$response) {
        die("Connection Failure.\n");
    }

    // Convert the result from JSON format to a PHP array
    $result = json_decode($response);
    if ( !is_object($result) ) {
        var_dump($response);
        die("Error handling result.\n");
    }
    if ( !isset($result->result_count) ) {
        die("Error: {$result->name} - {$result->description}\n.");
```

```
    }

    $options = '';
    foreach ( $result->entry_list as $entry ) {
        $options .= '<option value="'.$entry->id.'" >'.
        $entry->name_value_list->name->value.'</option>';
    }

    ?>
```

We'll build a string with a list of HTML option elements for each session in the returned list. This will enable the drop-down to select a session to rate to have the actual sessions right from your SugarCRM instance.

Figure 5-3. Session Feedback form

Now we need to handle the session feedback form submission. For this, we'll have another script that grabs the form data and posts it to the SugarCRM instance.

```php
<?php

// specify the REST web service to interact with
$url = 'http://localhost/~jmertic/ebook/service/v4/rest.php';

// Open a curl session for making the call
$curl = curl_init($url);

// Tell curl to use HTTP POST
curl_setopt($curl, CURLOPT_POST, true);

// Tell curl not to return headers, but do return the response
curl_setopt($curl, CURLOPT_HEADER, false);
```

```
    curl_setopt($curl, CURLOPT_RETURNTRANSFER, true);

    // Set the POST arguments to pass to the Sugar server
    $parameters = array(
        'user_auth' => array(
            'user_name' => 'myuser',
            'password' => md5('mypass'),
            ),
        );
    $json = json_encode($parameters);
    $postArgs = array(
                    'method' => 'login',
                    'input_type' => 'JSON',
                    'response_type' => 'JSON',
                    'rest_data' => $json
                    );
    curl_setopt($curl, CURLOPT_POSTFIELDS, $postArgs);

    // Make the REST call, returning the result
    $response = curl_exec($curl);

    // Make the REST call, returning the result
    $response = curl_exec($curl);
    if (!$response) {
        die("Connection Failure.\n");
    }

    // Convert the result from JSON format to a PHP array
    $result = json_decode($response);
    if ( !is_object($result) ) {
        var_dump($response);
        die("Error handling result.\n");
    }
    if ( !isset($result->id) ) {
        die("Error: {$result->name} - {$result->description}\n.");
    }

    // Get the session id
    $sessionId = $result->id;
```

Again, the usual login will be done to start things off. Now, we will simply create a new feedback record with the feedback form data POSTed to the script using the 'set_entry' method call.

```
    // Let's add a new Feedback record
    $parameters = array(
        'session' => $sessionId,
        'module' => 'pos_Feedback',
        'name_value_list' => array(
            array('name' => 'rating', 'value' => $_REQUEST['rating']),
            array('name' => 'description', 'value' => $_REQUEST['feedback']),
            ),
        );
    $json = json_encode($parameters);
    $postArgs = array(
```

```
                'method' => 'set_entry',
                'input_type' => 'JSON',
                'response_type' => 'JSON',
                'rest_data' => $json
                );
    curl_setopt($curl, CURLOPT_POSTFIELDS, $postArgs);

    // Make the REST call, returning the result
    $response = curl_exec($curl);
    if (!$response) {
        die("Connection Failure.\n");
    }

    // Convert the result from JSON format to a PHP array
    $result = json_decode($response);
    if ( !is_object($result) ) {
        var_dump($response);
        die("Error handling result.\n");
    }
    if ( !isset($result->id) ) {
        die("Error: {$result->name} - {$result->description}\n.");
    }

    // Get the newly created record id
    $feedbackId = $result->id;
```

Now, we need to associate the given Feedback record we just created with the passed Session record ID from the form to relate the Feedback given to a speaker's session. Just like before, we'll use 'set_relationship' for this.

```
    // Now relate the speaker to the session
    // Now let's relate the records together
    $parameters = array(
        'session' => $sessionId,
        'module_name' => 'pos_Feedback',
        'module_id' => $feedbackId,
        'link_field_name' => 'pos_sessions_pos_feedback',
        'related_ids' => array($_REQUEST['talk_id']),
        );
    $json = json_encode($parameters);
    $postArgs = array(
                'method' => 'set_relationship',
                'input_type' => 'JSON',
                'response_type' => 'JSON',
                'rest_data' => $json
                );
    curl_setopt($curl, CURLOPT_POSTFIELDS, $postArgs);

    // Make the REST call, returning the result
    $response = curl_exec($curl);
    if (!$response) {
        die("Connection Failure.\n");
    }

    // Convert the result from JSON format to a PHP array
```

```
$result = json_decode($response);
if ( !is_object($result) ) {
    var_dump($response);
    die("Error handling result.\n");
}

header('Location: feedbacksubmitted.html');
```

Overall, these customization scripts are straightforward to build, and should take any developer a matter of hours to begin delivering web forms that can push data to their SugarCRM instance or leverage data in the instance.

Summary

In this chapter, we learned all about SugarCRM's Web Services API, and saw some examples of how to use it with our conference application built on the SugarCRM platform. We created forms for enabled Attendee registration, speakers to send in their speaker abstracts, and to provide feedback on sessions, and linked these forms to our SugarCRM instance using PHP scripts designed to input the data using the SugarCRM Web Services API.

With this, we have built the components needed to enable our conference application to be used successfully. As with any application, the requirements will evolve over time, but the customizability and extensibility of the underlying platform, along with the ease of development thanks to the various developer tools, make the process painless, allowing the developer to concentrate on building the business logic and focus less on reinventing the wheel.

About the Author

John Mertic serves as the Community Manager for SugarCRM, having several years of experience with PHP web applications and open source communities. A frequent conference speaker and an avid writer, he has been published in php|architect, IBM Developerworks, and the Apple Developer Connection. He is also the author of the book *The Definitive Guide to SugarCRM: Better Business Applications* (Apress). He has also contributed to many open source projects, most notably the PHP project, where is the creator and maintainer of the PHP Windows Installer.

Colophon

The animal on the cover of *Building on SugarCRM* is a Honey Buzzard.

The cover image is from Wood's *Animate Creations*. The cover font is Adobe ITC Garamond. The text font is Linotype Birka; the heading font is Adobe Myriad Condensed; and the code font is LucasFont's TheSansMonoCondensed.

Get even more for your money.

Join the O'Reilly Community, and register the O'Reilly books you own. It's free, and you'll get:

- $4.99 ebook upgrade offer
- 40% upgrade offer on O'Reilly print books
- Membership discounts on books and events
- Free lifetime updates to ebooks and videos
- Multiple ebook formats, DRM FREE
- Participation in the O'Reilly community
- Newsletters
- Account management
- 100% Satisfaction Guarantee

Signing up is easy:

1. **Go to: oreilly.com/go/register**
2. **Create an O'Reilly login.**
3. **Provide your address.**
4. **Register your books.**

Note: English-language books only

To order books online:
oreilly.com/store

For questions about products or an order:
orders@oreilly.com

To sign up to get topic-specific email announcements and/or news about upcoming books, conferences, special offers, and new technologies:
elists@oreilly.com

For technical questions about book content:
booktech@oreilly.com

To submit new book proposals to our editors:
proposals@oreilly.com

O'Reilly books are available in multiple DRM-free ebook formats. For more information:
oreilly.com/ebooks

O'REILLY®

Spreading the knowledge of innovators   oreilly.com

The information you need, when and where you need it.

With Safari Books Online, you can:

Access the contents of thousands of technology and business books

- Quickly search over 7000 books and certification guides
- Download whole books or chapters in PDF format, at no extra cost, to print or read on the go
- Copy and paste code
- Save up to 35% on O'Reilly print books
- **New!** Access mobile-friendly books directly from cell phones and mobile devices

Stay up-to-date on emerging topics before the books are published

- Get on-demand access to evolving manuscripts.
- Interact directly with authors of upcoming books

Explore thousands of hours of video on technology and design topics

- Learn from expert video tutorials
- Watch and replay recorded conference sessions

CPSIA information can be obtained at www.ICGtesting.com
Printed in the USA
267193BV00001B/3/P